COMPLETE NO-FRILLS MEDITATION FOR AMERICANS ON-THE-GO

by

Wylie Smith

Cover by Steve McLachlin

Published by

REVEILLE BOOKS
Post Office Box 3114
Ormond Beach, FL 32175

Library of Congress Catalog # 89-64206

ISBN 0-9625090-2-7, $7.95 Softcover

Printed in United States of America

TABLE OF CONTENTS

Disclaimer

Nothing in this book should be construed as discouraging full use of the medical profession in care and treatment of disease, injury or other physical or mental disorders. Meditation is a valuable and proven method for building and maintaining sound health, bringing relief from pain and promoting healing and rapid recovery from disease. But no one should attempt its use to *supplant* medical care. Rather, the two should be staunch allies.

Modern doctors understand and encourage meditation. Indeed, their efforts follow very closely the meditators' "creed," full use of brain and mind to promote well-being of the human family. So consult your doctor whenever his/her services are needed. Then hasten the healing with meditation. And confide. You may be surprised to learn that he/she not only approves of meditation, but may actually BE a meditator!

BOOK ONE
BASIC MEDITATION

Introduction

"Why should I meditate?"

A fair question, but one with so many answers that I wrote the book on it. For starters, let's think about the following seven:

First and paramount, it is the most effective method ever devised for relaxing and shedding those excruciating tensions that literally kill hordes of hard-driving Americans each year.

Second, it's no tougher to learn and practice than the game of solitaire, yet it's infinitely more rewarding.

Third, it may be practiced anywhere, any time you can spare the few minutes that might otherwise be spent on a smoke or a soda.

Fourth, it does have side effects, all good.

Fifth, one of those is a change of personality and outlook to pure positive. Results: Dramatic improvement in business, social and personal relationships.

Sixth, it costs nothing.

Seventh, while certain groups have tainted the practice with connotations of voodooism and weird "religious" rites, you must remember that kooks are everywhere. Consider their raids on art and music. But in this book you will find no incense burning, chants, lotus or any other silly positions or contortions. Just relax in your favorite chair while using simple, scientifically selected procedures to soothe brain and mind by sending stress, tension, and their debilitating sidekicks, worry, fear, anger, hate and indecision, into precipitous retreat. Totally Americanized meditation for on-the-go Americans!

And those are just a few of the reasons you should meditate. For scads more, read on.

I

Fad or Revelation?

In the late '60s, a jolly little Indian guru began peddling meditation via TV talk shows. To most of us, the idea was as strange as was its genial purveyor. I thought it soon would be dead as the hula hoop. But years later I realized with a start that not only was it still around, it had changed the lifestyle of a fast-growing set of Americans. My writing instincts began clamoring: "What's with this thing? A story? Perhaps an expose?"

Early research turned up all manner of information, but very little on how to do. Most available material is scarcely more than promo. It took years of digging to get to the guts of meditation. And my biggest surprise—it works! It does indeed chase stress, tension, worry and related ills. But I also learned that most Americans are so turned off by cult ritual and required commitments of money, time and thinking, that they simply pass it up. And that's nothing short of tragic. So my most pleasant surprise was discovering that when we strip away meaningless rigmarole and bring in science and good old American common sense, it works even better!

Thus a story there certainly was, but not the one I expected. I found the urgent need was (and is) a no-frills, affordable course for thinking Americans. No dues or pledges, nothing to join or resign. Just enough time and mental energy to master a routine that will, *I* pledge, change your life. So here it is.

Sticking with science, when answers are unknown, we say so. Theories are so labeled. And since we will be dealing almost exclusively with mentality, let's begin with a short tour of the command post, the brain.

The Brain And Its Behavior

The human brain is divided into distinct hemispheres, left and right. One is emotional, adventurous, "ruled by the heart." The other is all business, "ruled by the head." And they never hesitate to make known their views. A sort of Tom and Dick Smothers' "Yes, it is," "No, it's not" skit going on inside your head, day and night, every day.

You need look no further than your own experiences to realize this "house divided" provokes indecision, then frustration, stress and, at times, illness. But that adversarial quality also serves a vital need. Rash ideas usually are overruled by sober second thoughts. Or, in an emergency, the more daring side takes over. It sends signals to glands that begin furiously pumping adrenalin and other natural drugs.

When our ancient forebears fought with bare hands or literally ran for their lives, those courage and stamina-building stimulants were lifesavers. But today, in our high-stress, low-activity society, the fight-or-flight pattern rarely is an option. In stress situations, we just sit and simmer. And that means trouble. Those powerful chemicals, unneeded and unused, seep into stomach and bloodstream, where they raise bloody hell. They bring on tension headaches, followed by bad temper and nervousness, then nausea and, finally, high blood pressure, ulcers or worse. So, as victims of an outmoded defense system, we are poisoned by the very juices that saved our ancestors.

We know strenuous exercise can work off some of those poisons. But many insist there's a better way— meditation. As you might guess, that claim has not gone unchallenged. Boston cardiologist Herbert Benson, with a research team, conducted scientific experiments on practicing meditators. His findings were startling.

Amazing Discoveries

Heart rate and oxygen consumption, old reliables for measuring relaxation, dropped some 20 percent in just three to five minutes. (Deep sleep, once believed most effective of all relaxers, takes five *hours* to bring an eight percent drop.) And note this: Normal blood pressure showed little change, but higher-than-normal dipped significantly.

Researchers were amazed. They and others demanded: "How?" Theorists suggested it had to do with totally soothing the brain, "synchronizing" its sides.

Further studies proved the synchronization theory correct. Freed from turmoil, brain sides relax and stop sending conflicting signals. Psychologists call the resulting mental state "slightly altered consciousness." Many meditators find it "euphoric." Whatever its name, results are astounding. Those poisons are somehow blocked or neutralized. And there goes your stress.

These surprising reports explain not only how the mind is drawn into a mildly altered state, but also how so wide an array of ailments is eliminated. They begin to vanish as secretions that caused them are sent packing. And they continue their retreat until another stressful situation brings them back. Then meditation once more will banish them. That's basic behavior of the brain, mind and body in meditation.

You Have Done A Form Of Meditation

It may surprise you to learn that you have done a sort of meditation, many times. Think not? Well, let's back up a bit. Remember your childhood, when Christmas was just around the corner? The pure joy, the ecstasy? You fairly tingled at the wonder of it all. And do you recall your first very own puppy or kitten? How about first love? You "danced down the street, a cloud at your feet." At such times, one's brain slips naturally into stressless harmony, no assistance needed. Results: Total relaxation, euphoria, plus lasting benefits. That is the heart, guts and goal of meditation. By whatever means, the aim is always that sense of total well-being brought on by brain synchronization. And the signal of its arrival is a gentle tingling.

The brain, you see, routinely sends out mild electric impulses, usually too weak to notice. But a synchronized brain sends synchronized impulses. They are strong enough to incite a pleasant tingling in the scalp, spreading to body and limbs. So when that begins, hang on to that totally relaxed condition. You're meditating!

COMMENTS AND QUERIES

These "Comments and Queries" sections are designed to serve two purposes. First, they should prod your memory and curiosity, cause a bit of extra thinking, and second, they allow you to express your own ideas, actually have an input in writing the book. Since we are dealing with meditation, a process that MUST be purely personal, what could be more normal and natural than your direct participation? Two blank pages are provided at the end of each chapter for that purpose. If you need more, tape or staple in extra sheets. You will find that writing out your thoughts and discoveries is the finest possible method for improving understanding and gaining new insights. I know. Long ago I learned the hard way that writing about a subject points up all too clearly how little we know of it!

Further, you will learn with ever more emphasis, that meditation is indeed strictly the personal matter we just mentioned. No two brains are identical. And since we are dealing almost totally with mentality, it is essential that you tailor your meditation to suit your special needs. Also, not only will YOU find such material helpful, so will any friends who may be fortunate enough to use such an updated volume. So thank you very much for your help!

Now for the business at hand, Comments and Queries.

Were you surprised to learn that you actually have two brains? Even if you were aware of it, perhaps pointing it out served to explain those indecisive times when half your being seems to be saying, "Go for it," while the other half seems just as intent on bringing you to an abrupt halt. Now you know what's going on and how to cope. MEDITATE!

And were you impressed with Dr. Benson's findings? You should be. They revolutionized thinking in the field of meditation. Never before had anyone proved scientifically that an actual change takes place in the brain when we meditate. "Slightly altered consciousness," to quote psychologists, or "euphoria," if we go with meditators' descriptions, now is recognized by science as a genuine physical and mental condition. Although they still know very little about it, there's no longer skepticism.

Also, while it may come as a shock to learn of the devastation wrought by those juices secreted when we are angry, fearful or worried, isn't it good to know that instant relief is available through meditation?

And finally, now that it has been pointed out, can't you recall many times when you "meditated?" Of course, you didn't recognize it at the time. But it was there. Remember?

Now jot down your own comments. Has the idea worked? Did it generate some additional thinking? If so, we're in business. You are well on the road to becoming a first-rate meditator! Congratulations!

NOTES

NOTES

II

Method Explored

While some lucky adults manage to retain the childhood gift of natural meditation, most of us lose it somewhere along the bumpy road to adulthood. We need an alternative. And who better qualified to teach Westerners than a 14th century English monk, who himself meditated several times each day? Just such an authority wrote an interesting book in which he expressed some very modern thinking. He remained anonymous, since he suggests ordinary mortals might contact God directly through prayer or meditation without benefit of clergy. In that day, such views were deemed rank heresy, grounds for a cookout with the heretic sizzling.

This portion, indeed, his entire book, should be read with the full knowledge that the monk lived in an age when dogma was sternly enforced by a harsh, unbending priesthood. Under such circumstances, he dared only hint at conflicting views. Yet remarkably, he is able to get across his unmistakable message of individual responsibility and rights. Please keep this in mind as you read his enlightening thoughts ahead.

Our brave monk called his book THE CLOUD OF UNKNOWING. In it he gives specifics for meditating. Obviously, he knew little of science. But he uses no trick coverups, either. As a monk, he cared nothing for comfort. His interests were spiritual. He nevertheless found in it "blessed peace and tranquility." We believe his basic method never has been improved. With wording slightly updated from Chaucerian Middle English, this is it.

The Monk's Method

He recommends as a first and most important step that you "choose one simple word your mind can easily recall, a word like God or love or any other that suits your taste . . . Clasp it in your mind so nothing may dislodge it. It must be your spear and shield in peace and war. With it, you shall clear away distracting thoughts, dropping them into the cloud of forgetting. If a thought continues to cling within you, demanding attention, answer with this one word alone. You must keep it whole. Do not break it up or analyze it. If you hold to this purpose, you may be sure disturbing thoughts will not remain. Why? Because you have refused to allow them to disrupt as you move forward in sweet meditation."

That's it. Simple, clear, succinct.

The "simple word" we are urged to clasp in our minds is the single most important item in bringing about the meditation mode. The good brother knew this. Note his appraisal: "It must be your spear and shield." This is an age when spear and shield could be one's only survival insurance. Then he advises: " . . . keep it whole. Do not break it up or analyze it."

Since the monk knew little of brain behavior (nor did anyone else of that age), the word's effects must have seemed weird, spooky, magic. Yet, unlike cults even to this day, he made no effort to cover such gaps in information with mumbo jumbo. Rather, he says in effect, "Enjoy the magic. We don't know why it works." That clearly was his intent when he advised, "Do not break it up or analyze it." In modern parlance, "Just use it. Don't mess around with it."

Here we see a typical example of basic differences in our approach and that of cults. We go with our monk's no-nonsense view that no stigma should attach to admitting we don't fully understand the brain. Learned scientists concede to this day that they have only tapped the tip of that marvelously complex apparatus. But how do cults deal with the word? As though it were black magic. They call it a mantra to suggest exotic mysticism, *they* select it and confer it on initiates through a haze of incense while chanting Sanskrit. And they warn their members never to divulge it to anyone. On and on goes the nonsense.

Choosing A Lull-Word

The purpose of the word/sound is to soothe or lull the brain, so we call it a "lull-word." And here we must turn briefly from our monk's selections to a process unheard of in his day. We learn through science that certain sounds are more soothing than others. One such is "a-h-h-h." Think about it. Truly, it is naturally soothing. We suggest you use it as your lull-word's first syllable. Studies also reveal that two-syllable sounds are more effective, the second giving a gentle nudge as it soothes. Those ending in "n," or "n" sounds, usually are most useful. So, with a-h-h-h-h as your first syllable, you might go through the alphabet for your second: bon, con, don, fon, etc. My choice is way down the abc's, ahh-von. But, to quote the monk, "Choose any word that suits your taste." As he indicated, words with special significance for you could prove more effective than scientifically selected sounds. Meditators vary widely. Some even use short phrases: Know thyself, love heals, etc. Anything that works is fine. However, unless you have good reason for selecting otherwise, we favor a-h-h-h-h sounds.

Obviously, the proper word or sound is priceless. You must use extreme care in your decision. Pronounce each prospective choice several times. And as you pronounce it, visualize it. How does it "feel?" What does it suggest? The "simple word" must be the only word. During meditation, it must lull you away from all else. It must please ALL senses, and disturb none.

Also, it is very important that every meditator choose his/her own lull-word. That is because a unique and ever-controlling background and personality dwells within each of us. What brings sad or unpleasant memories to me may have happy associations for you. That's a vital consideration. Discard any sound that evokes dark, dreary, depressing images. And give ample tests to those that bring forth light, airy, cheerful scenes. Also, nowhere is it carved in stone that you may not make as many changes as necessary to ensure the right choice. So experiment, try many. But once fully satisfied, you should hesitate to change. Do so only if you are convinced your choice was wrong. You see, eventually the sound must become an integral part of your makeup, as much a part of you as your name.

COMMENTS AND QUERIES

Well, what did you think of our 14th century English monk? Obviously a man well ahead of his time. And fortunately for us, deeply into meditation. We'll have a good deal more to say about him. And should you care to study his writings, Ira Progoff's fine book by the same name, THE CLOUD OF UNKNOWING, is available at libraries and book stores. For the original, you must go to the Library of Congress or possibly the library of a large university.

It is vital that you choose your lull-word carefully. As noted, this is the most effective tool ever developed for bringing on the meditation mode. So just follow instructions. Try many sounds or words, and only settle for one when you feel sure it is right for you. And even then, it's OK to change. It MUST be exactly YOUR word. Be patient. This chore may not be hurried.

This is one of our shortest chapters, but one of the most important. Please don't skim through it. Make *absolutely* certain that you have a lull-word that will serve you well.

And now, jot down your thinking. Please realize that this is an important exercise. It stamps into your consciousness, as nothing else can, the points that bother you, your work on them, and finally, your solutions. DON'T SKIP IT!

NOTES

NOTES

III

Ready to Begin

Now, with all necessary background information, you are ready to meditate. Find a quiet, semi-dark room, free from interruptions. Select a comfortable chair, but before taking your seat, loosen tight clothing and stretch luxuriously. Get comfortable. A fully relaxed body and mind are your best preparations. As you ease into your chair, roll your head in gentle circles, first in one direction, then the other. This head movement relaxes neck and shoulders and seems to aid the process.

Next, give yourself a short pep talk, something like: "I feel good about myself. I *know* good things happen to meditators." And why not feel good? You are entering a state that not only relaxes stress, it broadens and strengthens mentality, thereby opening wide avenues to a better life. You're taking charge of your life, your world. So show it. Be cheerful, happy. SMILE!

This is far more important than you can know. We'll get into it in detail later. But for now, just trust me. SMILE as you sit down to meditate. You must aim for and expect a mood closely approaching that of a child as Christmas nears. And you just can't find anything more exhilarating than that. You see, your smile isn't necessarily for things as they are, but for the way they're going to be. It has to do with faith in the outcome. And as you will soon see, this is one of meditation's most crucial, indeed, vital steps. So never forget, SMILE, AND MEAN IT!

Seated comfortably, relaxed, upbeat mood, you are all set. (Sit easily, comfortably, but don't slouch. That interferes with breathing, a very important factor.) Now, close your eyes and begin regular, moderately deep breathing. As you inhale, silently pronounce the first syllable of your lull-word, a-h-h-h-h. Then, as you exhale, say the second syllable, v-o-n-n-n (or whatever yours may be). If you have chosen a one-syllable word, repeat it, inhaling and exhaling. Or, if you use a phrase, compress it into two parts. Keep repeating, slowly, calmly, deliberately, timed to your breathing.

Now please don't simply mouth your word, as youngsters often do a catechism. You must relax, stay perfectly passive, but retain the image of your lull-word. Sense it moving into your brain, soothing, calming, bringing perfect harmony. And watch for signs of tingling. When they arrive, enjoy and go totally limp. That's the ONLY way to retain that euphoric sense. If other thoughts push into your consciousness, don't fret. Just turn your attention back to the lull-word.

Handling Bothersome Problems

One major problem while learning meditation is the tendency to tense up. You must watch for stress—back too rigid, pressing too hard on elbows, neck and shoulders tense—and correct it. Never, *NEVER,* **NEVER** try to force your will in meditation. Total passivity is a vital step in synchronizing your brain, thus allowing nature's positive forces to move in and take over. So go totally passive, but hold that cheerful smile!

Gradually, the process will become more and more natural, and finally, automatic. At that point, it is pure pleasure. But at first you must keep reminding, *RELAX.* Usually that is not too difficult, but you must be willing to put whatever effort is needed into learning the magic procedure.

In the beginning, your only aim is the mode. That is, the pleasant (some call it euphoric) sensation of detachment, mentally floating, carefree and totally relaxed. Just enjoy drifting through time and space. As your troubles drop away, float dreamily, happily, on Cloud Nine!

Once you are fully in the mode, drifting free of stress and care, stop your lull-word. Just enjoy. This is the aim of meditation. It is the time your brain and mind shed problems and rebuild energy, confidence and a sense of well-being. It is that euphoric period of rejuvenation. Enjoy, enjoy! When the mode fades, simply restart your lull-word. No problem.

And, as total relaxation takes over, booting out stress, your aches and pains will also vanish. Much pain is due directly to stress and all pain is worsened by it. So if you will mentally picture disease, illness and pain tied tightly to stress, as they literally are, what happens when stress is kicked out? They're gone! "As stress goes, so go the evils!"

Essentially, that's it. We slowly repeat our lull-word in time with breathing until we call up the mode. Then we enjoy total relaxation, realizing it is bringing relief from stress, tension, worry and associated ills. Sounds simple, and it is. But only if we thoroughly understand the method. So let's do a short recap.

A Look At Hypnosis

As we have seen, our lull-word is the most effective tool for bringing on the meditation mode. But it must be smoothly coordinated with all accompanying procedure. A quick look at hypnotists' methods might help. Some use a bright object to focus attention. And while the subject directs full attention to that, the hypnotist softly, gently, pleasantly and persuasively urges total relaxation, ceasing all thought, focusing only on the bright object. The aim, you see, is exactly the same as ours—totally harmonizing the brain. In that euphoric condition the mind is in a happy, positive state, eager to comply with suggestions.

Whether hypnosis actually is a deeper state than meditation makes little difference. Properly used, they both relax, provide therapeutic aid for mind and body, and can improve perception, comprehension and bring general mental enhancement. But meditation is always available, we need no help, and we never depart reality. Thus our preference for meditation. We can, however, apply some hypnotic techniques.

Note we suggest a pep talk as you begin meditation, and *demand* a smile. That's to work up the pleasure mood (whoever heard of a glum euphoria?). Next we stress total attention to your lull-word. (Better, we believe, than a bright object.) Stay relaxed but focus totally on that all-important word. With calm, pleasant but persuasive repetition, mentally watch as it slips into your mentality. The procedure soon becomes easy because it is so pleasant, just as is the hypnotist's persuasive intoning. So while meditation and hypnosis differ, they do share some features. Meditation enjoys the best, while discarding the objectionable.

Never Concentrate

A word here to clear up a fine shade of definition. You will notice that nowhere have we told you to "concentrate." *Focus* on your lull-word, but never concentrate.

There's good reason for this. Concentration requires mental exertion, direction, effort. That is exactly what we are striving to avoid, to leave behind.

I realize that telling you to focus, but not to concentrate, may seem a bit like saying, "Stand on your head, but keep both feet on the ground." Impossible. But not really. Concentration involves effort. Focusing, on the other hand, is the way a child relates to a security blanket, Teddy bear or some other old and trusted item with which he/she feels safe, comfortable and secure. The item is fully in the child's mind, almost to the exclusion of all else. This is precisely what your lull-word must be. Other things are all about, and both you and the child know it. But nothing is important enough to disrupt that special relationship. Random thoughts drift in and out of your mind. That's natural and desirable. Only when a thought or idea persists and grows do you need a bit of extra focusing on your lull-word. Hopefully, that clears up the subtle difference and explains why we focus but NEVER concentrate.

"Tingling" Explained

We keep referring to "tingling" as a sign that the meditation mode has arrived. As noted, it is caused by strengthened but still faint electric impulses from a brain in sync. Don't expect a shock. It is so feeble, in fact, that you easily could miss it. We call it tingling, but that may not seem apt to you. Einstein spoke of it as "a special feeling in the tips of my fingers." Many call it euphoria. It is closely akin to that sense of well-being you felt on special occasions as a child. So if tingling doesn't quite describe your feelings, you nevertheless should recognize whatever special feeling you have. Next to your lull-word, and directly linked with it, that special feeling is most important. Indeed it IS meditation. Watch for it CAREFULLY!

And let's make one more determined effort to stamp into your consciousness the absolute necessity for total passivity, mental and physical. The temptation, especially at first, is to concentrate into the mode. DON'T TRY IT. It won't work. You must be a receiving set, not a generator. So with your lull-word, coax a condition of absolute relaxation. Then, and only then, can the tingling begin, signaling that the two brain sides are in sync, thus allowing that stress-chasing, delightful healing of tension-wracked mind and body.

I suppose the reason some Americans find this so difficult is that we are accustomed to pouring all our energy and enthusiasm into whatever we do. In my own case, I learned to meditate and thought I was enjoying its full benefits. But months later, by accident, I discovered I hadn't really been letting go fully. I had been reserving a bit of energy, presumably to "push" my desires for reaching the mode. When I finally learned to release every vestige of control, to go limp, be a wet rag, a glob of Jello, my enjoyment and benefits increased many fold.

Some teachers use another analogy: "Nature hates a vacuum." So when you cease all activity and vacate your mind of conscious thought, nature's soothing, healing forces are promptly drawn in to clean up the mess left by stress, worry, fear and hate. Don't make it difficult by building energy barriers.

"Full" Meditation Sessions

We have stressed that meditation may be practiced anywhere, any time. All experienced meditators use short "med breaks" to ease tension and relax mind and body several times each day. But they also do "full" sessions (at least 15, preferably 20 minutes) twice daily. Most find just after rising and before retiring natural periods for setting a cheerful, relaxed mental and physical state. But any time that's convenient is fine. Very soon, that quiet, peaceful retreat becomes a time to look forward to, a highlight of the day.

These longer sessions are vital, not only because they are more effective at relaxing near term, but because it is from such prolonged interludes in the meditation mode that lasting benefits derive. Real and meaningful health improvement, expanded mental capacity, a better, more cheerful outlook and attitude toward others, in short, a better life in every way, is the palpable result of 20-minute, twice-daily meditation. You may feel that you simply can't spare the time. But be assured, once you have seen results, you will pass up sleep or just about anything else to get in your full meditating. Trust me, you can't afford *not* to.

You Must Get The Message

If I have repeated instructions to the point of redundancy, I apologize. On second thought, no, I don't. There's an old saw kicking around the advertising business, "Tell 'em what you're going to tell 'em, tell 'em, tell 'em what you told 'em." Ad folk know repetition annoys. But they also know we remember things that annoy. And since getting the meditation message across is vital, top priority, a MUST, I apologize only if I *haven't* annoyed. Please read, reread, then read again. And try it each time. Once you reach the mode, boredom, annoyance and other cares that infest the day will fold their tents in the night, and silently steal away.

COMMENTS AND QUERIES

This is a long chapter, and may at first seem rather involved. However it is devoted entirely to the most important single item in all the field of meditation bringing on the "mode" through use of your lull-word. You must fully realize that the meditation mode is the basis for all meditating, of whatever nature or depth. Thus it is vital that you master the process. But have no fear. It's quite simple and easy. There is just one requisite—total relaxation and passivity.

Has it given you trouble? Well, that's natural too. You see, we Americans are so gung-ho on instant results that we tend to push too hard, concentrate on a problem, then get results or blow our top. Meditation doesn't work that way. It is precisely the other end of the spectrum. Successful meditation is perfect relaxation, allowing the good things to come to us. So we never *do* anything. But the mode, in which our brain is in complete harmony, thus perfectly relaxed, synchronized, invites all those wondrous gifts of nature to enter and take charge. So if you have experienced difficulty, not to worry. Rather, just stretch out, relax and LET it happen. Once you learn to relax, it will. So keep trying. It's quite easy. but you must get over that impulse to take charge and MAKE it happen!

You should have quite a bundle of comments at this point. This is one of our most important chapters and very few readers come through without some difficulty. So write 'em down. Think about them. Then go back and read about them. But don't get discouraged. You're coming now to the point where meditation becomes what it is meant to be—pure fun!

NOTES

NOTES

IV

That's It!

That, my fortunate friend, is the total technique. There are, of course, many branches of meditation. But it all must begin with achieving and using the mode. And you hold here the most effective method for doing so ever devised. I wonder if you fully appreciate your rare treasure? What price can one place on relaxation, on easy and readily available relief from pain? And those are just the more obvious benefits. Side effects such as quicker grasp and deeper comprehension, wider ranging interests in people, places and events, and greater capacity to enjoy will emerge slowly but surely. As its ever-increasing help becomes more evident, you will one day realize your new-found skill is priceless!

PLEASE, however, UNDER NO CIRCUMSTAN-CES, become discouraged if your first tries are not successful. The simple process is, after all, a learning experience. Also, it involves retraining the brain. And that, for most of us, is a brand new direction. It may take time. Your first few sessions may bring only calming, slightly rested feelings. That's OK. It's a start. When you feel floating and drifting, that's progress. And when you finally feel tingling, you have arrived. You're meditating.

In the unlikely event that after a half dozen or so tries, you feel nothing at all, something is wrong. Try another lull-word. Some just will not work for everyone. If you still have no success, write me. Send details and a self-addressed, stamped envelope. I'll give it personal attention.

What To Expect

Now that you are a full-fledged meditator, what should you expect for your trouble? Well, quite a few things, but not all at once. You should begin to note a distinct improvement in health, physical and mental. Your lifestyle, both at work and play, should be more relaxed, laid-back, more enjoyable. And your relations with others, oh yes, definitely including your sex life should move markedly ahead.

In the mental field, you should be growing progressively more perceptive, and enjoying it more. Little things that used to annoy you or were simply ignored, now interest and please you. Your new-found perception will lead to more comprehension and retention. And of course, the most striking gain is the one that attracted you in the first place, ridding your body and mind of stress, tension and the multiple evils they bring on. Actually, all these other benefits are due to conservation of energy and directing it into new, positive areas. It takes an enormous amount of strength and energy to worry, dread, hate, cope with indecisiveness and other ills caused by stress and tension. Now you are using that heretofore wasted power to build the sort of life you used to dream of.

Don't leave it to chance. Now that you realize you have the capabilities and stamina to bring about new attainments, step out and take charge. Make new friends, take on new assignments, make it clear to your boss or business associates, friends and family, that you are a new, dynamic person, capable of doing more for them, for your company and for yourself.

Those are just a few of the benefits that await you. Keep your eyes and mind open for the many, many more. Don't let them slip away, as non-meditators might!

A "Gee Whiz" Bonus

And one final reward for those who have diligently coaxed brain and mind this far:

Dr. Howard Gardner, Harvard University psychologist, has concluded from extensive research that we all have at least seven types of intelligence. Further, he believes genius consists not so much of super intellect as in ability to move easily from one type of brain power to others, thus gaining new perspectives and concepts. He is convinced that great thinkers, daVinci, Edison, Einstein and many others, all had this "mental fluidity." Other scientists support his findings.

This is an intriguing discovery for meditators. A synchronized brain doesn't snap like a rubber band, back into two feuding sides. Each time you meditate, your brain slips more easily into sync and remains longer. And in that happy state, access to all types of intelligence obviously becomes easy and natural. So, if Dr. Gardner is right and you have no serious objections, just relax, keep meditating and prepare for your manifest destiny—genius!

Meantime, HAPPY MEDITATING!

COMMENTS AND QUERIES

Well, by now you should feel pretty good about yourself. You have mastered the basics of meditation or are well on the way. And that means that you no longer are a slave to stress, tension and their camp-followers: worry, fear, hate and incentive-destroying indecision. You now are in the driver's seat. You control your destiny. If that doesn't send shivers of excitement dancing up and down your spine, better have the old spine checked.

But don't be alarmed or discouraged if you are not yet totally proficient in bringing on the mode and enjoying full benefits. We have stated repeatedly that meditating is a simple procedure. And it certainly is. But so is an easy game like solitaire or blackjack. Yet both take some study and experience. And so does meditating. However, each time you sit down to a session you will gain more ease, effectiveness and enjoyment. And before you know it, your meditating will be just what we have called it, pure fun!

No doubt you will have a fairly wide range of remarks to write out at this stage. That's fine. In reviewing, they will be of great help. It is so easy to forget our early struggles once we have become thoroughly comfortable with a new subject. So don't spare the ink. Is a certain phase giving you problems? How have you attempted to cope? Has the effort been successful? Could the subject have been presented more clearly, in order to avoid these problems? Lay it on the line. And once you have finished the course, I'd like to hear from you. I'm most anxious to improve the next printing.

And finally, it should be noted that even if you go no further, you now have a skill that will bring almost instant relief from stress, tension and all the devastating evils they bring on. In their place will come harmony, increased vigor and stamina, and amazing new incentives and opportunities for a better life in every way. In short, you've got it made. CONGRATULATIONS!

NOTES

NOTES

BOOK TWO
MEDITATION'S DEEPER SIDE

Introduction

Meditation is an export to the West from the "Mysterious East." That's hardly surprising. We know civilization reached a high level on that part of the planet while still struggling to gain a few tenuous beachheads in Europe. And very early records disclose Eastern monks, scholars and others as advanced meditators. Also, it is not surprising that considerable Eastern influence has clung to the practice.

Much of that exotic flavor consists of chants, body "positions" and other customs usually designed to honor and commemorate ancient gurus. We can under stand such desires and resulting ritual. However, to most Westerners, such acts are no more meaningful than sitting cross-legged and miserable while reciting senseless doggerel.

So, with all due deference to honorable ancients, we choose to skip it. Thus, we have stripped away those annoying coats of rigmarole but have scrupulously left untouched basic theories and practices. For thousands of years they have proved their worth. So as we master their meanings and learn procedures long used with amazing results, it is no idle boast to state that new dimensions to life await just ahead.

But first let's take a moment to look at where we are and where we wish to go.

Meditation's Many Faces

One of meditation's most appealing aspects is its many widely diverse facets. Truly, it offers something for everyone. Thousands use it, in the words of one writer, as a "giant aspirin tablet." They find its relaxing, stress- and tension-chasing features fully satisfying and see no need to explore further. Their goal is reached. And what's wrong with that? Many others, however, find in it far deeper substance. Surely no one can fault that worthy aim, either. But certain safeguards should be observed.

It is advisable, for example, that one not begin serious participation in this segment until he/she is a thoroughly experienced, competent meditator. Advanced meditation is, by its very nature, totally personal. To be effective, one must adapt it to fit his/her unique background, experience and concepts. And that requires full proficiency in its mechanics. Quickly achieving the mode and holding it easily must be almost automatic in order that full focus may be directed toward more challenging aspects. When you have reached that stage, welcome. But please spend enough time on basic meditation to assure that you are ready to move on. After all, ample rewards are found at any level. No need to reach too far too fast.

Important note: Advanced meditation is much more than the act of meditating. It is a total lifestyle. Therefore, we must assume a willingness to adapt to new concepts. But don't be alarmed. Notice we said "adapt," not "adopt." Basically, this means learning, then living in complete harmony with nature and nature's forces of the universe. And any reasonable person should find that an easy, pleasant assignment. No commitments, no acceptance of objectionable concepts, nor rejection of any of yours. Rather, it entails nothing more than gearing your present views to new discoveries. It's exciting and SO rewarding. One further important plus, it helps make meditation what you learned to expect in your basic studies—pure fun!

I

Basic Concepts

Obviously, all Eastern meditators do not share all the following beliefs. So widespread a practice naturally has many divergent avenues. Our intent, therefore, is to offer a wide-angle picture, broad enough to include those basic perceptions that have proved of great value, while omitting details that tend to separate. Of course we drop all ritual and non-essentials.

Some of the following may come as a bit of a shock. In view of their importance, however, we must not soften or change. So please just read and consider. No need to pass judgment.

This first idea is a widely accepted Eastern philosophical concept, especially among meditators. Basically it holds that all things, animate or inanimate, animal, human or spiritual, are directly linked to everything else. In short, all the universe is one entity. It is often called the "total oneness" theory.

An astonishing aspect of this idea is that it has been part of meditation's tradition since ancient times. No one knows for how many thousands of years monks, scholars and others have embraced it. Also, for many years Western theoretical thinkers have affirmed a similar belief in a unified universe. And it was Einstein's greatest disappointment that he could never put together a formula that would logically and mathematically prove a viable connection between all things. He was certain such links exist. Try as he did, however, over many years, he could never come up with hard evidence.

Now, physicists working in quantum mechanics believe they are on to a theory that may do exactly that. They call it "superunified theory of the universe." It is far too complex to tackle here, but in the minds of many it is the coming together of science, religion and philosophy. And how have meditators known of this strange phenomenon for thousands of years? Welcome to one more of meditation's vast store of mysteries!

The Basic Field Of Energy

Another fundamental perception from out of the East is a firm conviction that a vast "sea" of pure energy engulfs us all, indeed permeates the entire universe. This, say its proponents, is the realm of spirits and/or forces of the universe, known and unknown. Also, its amazing properties make possible instant transference of thought waves, from any distance. And guess what: Scientists now are debating the theory of a universal energy field!

These two widely held Eastern concepts underlie much of the thinking and practice of advanced meditation. They are so vital, in fact, that you must stamp them into your memory bank. That is not to say you must accept them. But just as your knowledge of history and geography help you with current events, so these will help steer your perception of deeper aspects of meditation.

The Spirit World—Eastern Version

Any venture into the realm of spirits is so misty a trek through obviously unknown territory, it seems far safer to stick with indications of their presence, rather than spirits *per se*. That generally is the course of Eastern writers, and I mean to follow their wise lead. For your information, however, let us take a quick look at perceptions that play so large a part in much of Eastern thought and behavior.

One such concept holds that the Great Spirit Body consists of many spirits, gathered, perhaps merged, but still maintaining individual identity. This is in keeping with the total-unity theory, that all spirits are interrelated. Also it is believed that all operate within the same natural laws that control the rest of the universe. This obviously brings the spirit domain into much closer relationship with our physical world than does the conventional Western view. Thus contacts, communication and help must be closer. Also, it may boar diroctly on the widely held theory of reincarnation.

But in the East, as in the West, few if any beliefs are universally accepted. However, a theory that may be more widespread than realized holds that as human comprehension expands, many current concepts will be discarded as overly simplistic. And final understanding of total truth will bring all beliefs and perceptions into one compatible entity.

Now that Western science has shown that we currently use only a tiny portion of our brain, this theory may not cause quite the stir in the West that might once have been the case. At any rate, it offers an acceptable compromise in the East.

Natural Law—Eastern Style

Although many Easterners believe everything, including creative intelligence, is subject to natural law, they, too, have their miracles and supernatural happenings. They explain these, however, as not really "super," or above the laws of nature. Rather, they say such things do conform to those laws, but operate in parts of that system not yet fully understood.

Perhaps it should come as no surprise that a concept that puts such emphasis on natural law and natural processes in all forms of existence should approach "worship" in a somewhat more natural manner than does the West. Much of Eastern philosophy regards full use of one's mentality as the only true homage to the Great Spirit Body. The human brain, so goes the thinking, was not developed to languish behind curtains of greed, expedience or indolence. So fine an instrument is meant for use, for making genuine contributions to the human family. And that, it is believed, is the highest display of reverence that may be paid an intelligence capable of engineering and managing the universe.

While it may not fit our conventional Western training, we must admit it does have certain logical appeal.

And now, having learned basic thinking throughout much of the East, may we offer a suggestion? Don't accept or reject. Simply lay it aside in a corner of your mentality and let it "simmer." In meditation, as noted above, there is no pressure to accept anything. Just know of it, give it some thought, then at some unexpected moment, it may come to mind and bring with it a clearer perception and/or understanding. That's the way these knotty problems often resolve themselves, without accepting, rejecting, or even putting any conscious effort into the matter. One more of the limitless wonders of meditation.

Your Own Spirit

Now, since we are on the subject of spirits, we may as well go straight into one of the most important features of all meditation, your own spirit.

Your spirit (mind) is vital to every decision of whatever size or nature, from batting an eyelash to planning and executing invasion of a continent. While pitifully little is known about it, every student of human anatomy knows that the brain is the body's command post. In some mysterious fashion, the mind is closely associated with and apparently the activator and director of that marvelous piece of equipment. So what could be more important? Yet the total mind is so misunderstood and is called by so many misleading names that few of us seem to have a clear concept of its true nature. We believe it is so vital that the next chapter will deal with it exclusively. Be prepared for surprises, all amazingly good.

Having considered the foundation blocks of Eastern meditation, perhaps you are growing restive.

"When," you may ask, "are we going to meditate?" Well, why not now? You see, advanced meditation differs from the basic type only in attitude. You are now aware of the long-held Eastern concepts that, while you may never adopt, you may one day adapt. And therein you may discover the strength and amazing powers of deeper meditation. So why not begin? At this point the only new tool you might employ is a deeper relaxation, a more complete passivity. Since advanced meditation seeks outside help, total openness and receptivity are necessary. They can be achieved only through absolute relaxation.

So go right ahead. Meditate whenever you please. I predict that even at this early stage, you will be pleasantly surprised at the more meaningful, in-depth sense of expanded gains your new perceptions will impart. No need to consciously bring them into your sessions. A subliminal or barely conscious awareness is enough. Therefore, meditating as you learn, using each additional bit of information to increase your effectiveness, is an excellent idea. Watch for the gradual but very real growth in genuine achievement and pleasure. Enjoy your mental expansion as it takes place!

COMMENTS AND QUERIES

This is an important chapter in view of its subject matter, basic beliefs of Eastern meditators. Also, it introduces the recommended approach to new or unfamiliar material.

Meditators traditionally are open minded, willing, even anxious to learn of new ideas. But that does not mean they accept anything, merely because it's new. It is rare, however, to hear a meditator exclaim, "That's ridiculous." Far more likely is the comment, "That's an interesting thought." It may then be relegated to some remote corner of mentality, never again to be called up. Or it may be brought back frequently, mulled over, perhaps eventually accepted. But obviously an open mind is vital. Any other approach automatically shuts out ALL new thinking. Thus our advice: Neither accept nor reject on first contact. Just stow it away for future reference. Time and experience may alter your outlook. Anyway, what harm can it do to know of new ideas?

I'm sure you found some of the Eastern thinking unusual. So it is important to keep the above in mind. Since ther ideas in question have served so admirably for thousands of years, we certainly should not reject them out of hand. But neither need we accept anything we find troubling. Just file it away, as suggested. That's the meditator's way.

It would be interesting to have a look at notes on this chapter. I'll bet they are widely varied and all interesting!

And now be prepared for perhaps the most important aspect of all meditation your own spirit. In this you should have no trouble adapting. But read on. Wonderful surprises await!

NOTES

NOTES

II

Your Spirit

This is a subject we can all identify with, and one in which we desperately need greater involvement, our mind. We casually speak of the mind as though everyone knows all about it. But just ask someone to define it. The plain fact is, no one, including scientists who study it, can say precisely what it is. And even among the most knowledgeable, there is wide disagreement. Psychologists have long known it is divided into "conscious" and "subconscious." The conscious, or surface section, is used for daily living. The subconscious is deeper, more difficult to reach. It stores, say scientists, everything we ever experienced.

Meditators agree that the "other mind" is a ready source of information. But most believe its supply is much greater than science has ascribed. They think that as a link with higher levels, it is privy to *all* information.

Whether or not we accept that thinking, we must agree that the mind is an amazing piece of equipment. Also, most of us would have to admit that we use only a tiny fraction of its multi-faceted faculties. So, beyond doubt, we should get better acquainted, the sooner the better.

For so powerful an entity, one that acts in total obscurity, what an apt analogy we find in the fabled genie imprisoned in a bottle. You will recall he could only perform his marvelous feats when released.

So it is with your deeper mind or spirit. Powerful though he is, he can only assist when you call him out of the bottled-up recesses of your consciousness. And how do we call him? Meditators have an easy, built-in method, effective, and always available. Just tie in the call with your lull-word. In my case, I call my spirit *Von*, the second syllable of my lull-word, *a-h-h-h-h Von*. Thus, whenever I begin my meditation, my spirit is called in with the mode. It works.

This practice makes sense for several reasons. As you know, in synchronizing the brain, we also soothe our entire mind, making it available and ready to serve, rather than being tied up with the stress and tension of a normal lifestyle. But to think and deal with it in terms of "the mind," is awkward. It is much easier and natural to use an allegorical symbol and give a name to further personify him.

This is so important a step that I believe it warrants a bit more space and time. As noted, no one can fully define the mind. My dictionary gives an even dozen definitions, the most appropriate, it seems to me, being the Greek root word, *menos*, meaning "spirit" (what else?). Think about it. Your mind can soar into space with Carl Sagan, probe deep seas with Jacques

Cousteau, drift back in time or jet into the future. It goes where only a spirit may venture. So what more appropros than the "spirit" designation?

Your Spirit's Vast Powers

Perhaps an even closer representation than the genie is found in Shakespeare's plays. In THE TEMPEST, we meet a delightful "airy spirit," Ariel, and his master, Prospero. Hear Ariel's salute to his master: "I come to answer thy best pleasure, be it to fly, to swim, to dive into fire, to ride on the curl'd clouds, to thy strong bidding, task Ariel and all his quality."

Could we ask a better characterization? Shakespeare obviously had a close working relationship with his spirit. He knew his wondrous talents!

That brings up an interesting point. Over and over in Eastern literature, we find the admonition, "Look deep within thyself." Western writers phrase it more succinctly, "Know thyself." And we need not remind that this current generation is obsessed with "finding myself," discovering "who I am."

What do all these probes into the depths of oneself hope to discover? Why has the quest seemed of such vital importance to deep thinkers and writers for thousands of years? There can be but one answer. The search deep within is a response to the burning urge to explore the soul, mind, spirit.

The fact that so many of such varied types have realized the importance of knowing one's spirit should serve as an added incentive for meditators. We have a decided advantage. Not only do we know exactly what we seek, we also know how to reach our spirit. So let's waste no time in availing ourselves of his vast powers!

Please get over any qualms you may have over personifying your mind as a spirit to better grasp and use it. This is no upstart idea, nor is it exclusively Eastern. Western literature is full of such references. How about a quote from Jesus? Mat. 26:41, "The spirit indeed is willing but the flesh is weak."

Further, as we have shown clearly, the deeper mind IS a spirit. He is that "still, small voice," warning of danger ahead, he is your conscience, your guardian angel, the Muse writers "woo for inspiration," the Lady Luck gamblers beseech, an "inner eye," a "sixth sense," and many, many more. No matter how perceived or what he is called, he's one and the same, your spirit. And many meditators believe his most important function is providing your link with higher levels and the limitless potential such ties imply. So please, put your qualms to rest and your spirit to work!

How To Reach Him

Begin by tying in your lull-word, as suggested. As you repeat it, you must actually feel his presence, a tangible being you are calling into your consciousness. This is an ideal place to learn "blending," a practice you will find useful through much of your meditating.

Let's start by fully understanding the meaning of the word. As used here, blending refers to total fusion, merging, becoming a part. As when an artist blends colors to form a desired "blend," leaving no trace of the original. Merely mixing is not enough. Blending is truly becoming one in spirit.

When we call up spirit, that must be our aim, to blend. We must totally open our mentality, cease all resistance. Then feel and "see" his blending as we might watch a heavy fog roll in off the sea. Its density blocks out all else. And in some mysterious fashion peculiar to thick fog, we seem actually to become part of it. That's blending. And remember, the fog came to you, you didn't go to it. So it must be with all blending. Just open completely and ALLOW it to happen.

This is not nearly as difficult as it may sound. You have learned to relax and lay open your total being. Now you are applying that practice to one of its most important assignments. Just be sure you achieve *complete* relaxation and passivity.

A sure sign that you and spirit are indeed blending is a deeper mode, a more complete release from stress and tension, and a more realistic drift. This may require a few practice sessions, but it is so enjoyable it should not only be well worth the effort, but pure fun as well!

What You May Expect

As spirit answers your call and becomes a part of your daily life, it is very important that you know not only what to look for, but what *not* to expect. You may very soon begin to realize quite suddenly that you know things you can't recall learning. Solutions to problems may slip quietly into your consciousness. Many meditators are convinced that's spirit at work. Of course, your meditations in larger matters, too, may be fully satisfying. But that quiet, barely noticeable help in everyday routines seems a hallmark of our spirit.

Strange as it may seem, there's nothing really strange about it. After all, spirit is part of you and always has been. I suspect he arrives with the lull-word even in basic meditation. Since newcomers are not ready for spiritual involvement, we refrained from mentioning it. But when you feel "tingling" and know the mode has arrived, so has spirit! So, although you only now have become aware of his presence, you actually have experienced it many times. Thinking back, you may recall such instances. At the time, perhaps you vaguely wondered about them. Now you *know* what's happening.

But don't look for drums and trumpets announcing his arrival. His is quiet, subdued help, no jolts or shoves, just gentle nudges. Although he is with you at all times, his presence is SO easy to overlook. And never forget, his help is optional. He'll never force you into anything. Final decisions are yours, ALWAYS.

Short Review

Now a quick rundown to ensure that you fully grasp and rely on spirit. As noted, we seem to have two minds. No one can fully understand either, let alone both. But when we call up spirit, we are reaching and including in our meditation that part of the mind psychologists call the "subconscious." They often attempt, with varying degrees of success, to call it into play through hypnosis. So while they may not accept our evaluation, that through spirit *all* knowledge is available, they do know and all agree that his help is real. And let's not forget that for thousands of years, Eastern meditators have used his services with amazing results.

So, if you have had misgivings, better send them packing. Since not only the ancients, but skeptical, modern scientists accept and stand in awe of his powers, could anything be more ill advised than doubting his being? Don't treat a great and good friend in any such shabby fashion. Especially when he stands at your threshold, loaded with wondrous gifts!

One important note definitely must be called to your attention. We have stressed the importance of your lull-word. Now you see clearly its vital part in your meditation. It is your link with spirit, his name, his call to join you in bringing soothing relaxation and help in every trying situation. As such, it is truly priceless, not only practical, but spiritual in significance. Realization of these facts should make the word and subsequent mode not only easier to use, but far more meaningful, a fully personal item. And now you are in truth entering the field of advanced meditation. Welcome!

COMMENTS AND QUERIES

Another important chapter and one I earnestly hope you will commit to memory and understanding. The idea of a personal spirit may come as a revolutionary idea, perhaps even a shock, accustomed as we are to strictly pragmatic thinking. But we must remember that meditation is an ancient and amazingly successful method for achieving a better life. And it works through utilization of help not available to most, higher levels of mentality. So isn't it perfectly normal and natural that we call in our direct link with that realm, our very own spirit? As we have seen, some most impressive authorities find the concept fully acceptable. It may take a bit of adjusting, but be assured, whatever effort is involved, results are well worth it!

Be sure to write out your early feelings on this (for most) radical idea. Such thinking will be helpful to you and very useful to anyone who reads your book later. What were your initial reactions? How did you cope? Did you meditate, permit the solution to gradually filter into your being? That's a very good method. But what was yours?

We will look further into the spirit world. But our own spirit is the only one we'll deal with directly and unequivocally as a spirit. As noted, in matters totally theoretical, we carefully avoid specific claims. But, as you will soon discover, there can be no doubt of the existence and close proximity of our own spirit!

NOTES

NOTES

III

Meditation and Religion

There has always been considerable confusion in the West as to meditation's relation to religion. Indeed, many non-meditators firmly believe it is "just another Eastern religion." Charlatans have turned this into an advantage, carefully tailoring Eastern practices to their own purposes. If they can inject religious connotations, so much the better.

The truth is, meditation bears very much the same relation to religion as does prayer. It is important to many faiths, East and West, but no more the property of any ono porouasion than is prayer, music, art, or for that matter, Bingo or pot luck suppers. But since it has always been so closely identified with Eastern "holy men," let us take a closer look.

Buddhist monks universally are meditators. That is no coincidence. And since Buddhism certainly is one of, if not the most widely practiced religions throughout much of the East, it seems an excellent starting point.

A Look At Buddhism

Siddhartha Guatama was born about 560 B.C. into a wealthy Hindu family. His early years were spent in easy, perhaps riotous living, with no thought for the impoverished masses of India. Then, at about age 30, he had a "vision" while meditating. It turned his life around and he began at once to preach his new gospel.

This was a radical departure from widely accepted Vedic law. It discarded doctrines of caste, priesthood, theology and ritual. In their place, he taught compassion and love for all mankind, indeed, for all living things. He viewed the welfare of all as the concern of all. (How like the teachings of Jesus!) His followers bestowed the reverent title of Buddha (Enlightened One) on him.

These humane and gentle views are widely reflected in perceptions and practices of Eastern meditators. Therefore, it usually is assumed that they were lifted from Buddhism. But were they?

Buddhism, remember, was born of meditation. So we know the Buddha was a meditator. No doubt he had spent weeks, months, perhaps years, discussing practices, thinking and aims with other learned meditators. And it well may be that it was from these contacts that his doctrine took shape. Who can say for how many thousands of years these lofty goals had been pursued in meditation? So while meditation and Buddhism do indeed move in strikingly parallel paths, isn't it more likely that Buddhists learned from meditators, rather than the other way around?

(We should point out that Buddhism has taken so many directions that some forms bear little resemblance to original teachings. Myth, strange gods and practices have completely diverted its message in many lands. Only in small pockets in Burma, Thailand and Sri Lanka are said to be among the very few places it is practiced in something close to early form.)

And Now, Westward

Let's turn now to the West, back to our 14th century English monk to whom we owe so much of our meditating technique. He has a great deal to say on this phase of the subject, some of it downright amazing in its perception of matters one would think he had no way of knowing anything about. After all, he was cloistered away in an English monastery, supposedly completely out of touch with things Eastern. Yet he—but let's move on. You be the judge.

His book is aimed at all who feel the need for a "personally proven" religion. A surprisingly modern approach, and a dangerous one in that day.

The book's title, THE CLOUD OF UNKNOWING, describes a condition in which man is separated, but at the same time joined with his God by a state of mind. In order to change the cloud from "separated from" into a "link with" one's God, man must somehow drop concepts that tend to distance him from his God. Obviously, he is counseling meditation, in which one coaxes the brain into synchronized bliss, oblivious to normal cares and preconceived forms, tenets or other perceptions. And in this state of mind, our monk states, "sudden stirrings, instantly springing toward God," will occur. He believes this is so because it "is the work of God alone."

The Monk's Approach

Then he states that "naked man" must approach his "naked God," alone through the "cloud of darkness and unknowing." Obviously, he is flouting conventional belief that man needs priestly intercession. Clearly, "naked man" is without benefit of organized religion's prescribed ritual and dogma, and "naked God" is shorn of all traditional trappings one is taught to expect. He goes on to describe the behavior of the determined seeker:

"In desperation he cries out, 'God, God, God, God.' If this short prayer is uttered in height, depth, length and breadth of spirit, it reaches God. And God replies. Short prayers enter heaven."

Do you see what he is doing? He has taken the word he recommends first as a lull-word (" . . . God, love or any other") and used it both to bring on the meditation mode, and as a fervent prayer. Thus he actually fuses prayer and meditation.

So in the monk's case, meditation indeed is a real and important part of his religion. But that is a purely personal application. As he stresses over and over throughout his book, meditation, and indeed religion as well, must be totally personal with subtle nuances and meanings unique to each individual.

The monk doesn't go much beyond this point. Why should he? If God "replies," his goal is reached. His meditation/prayer is answered.

In that day of stylized worship of an aloof, virtually unapproachable God, such teaching must have seemed radical indeed. Far closer to the Eastern concepts of a spirit world with direct personal ties to humanity. Finding the "God that is," rather than one we have been taught exists, has a distinctly Eastern flavor.

The ultimate goal of dedicated Eastern meditators is enlightenment. That is, reaching and establishing communion with the Source. Could we find a more cogent description of Western perception of the Source than the "God that IS?" And our monk is saying that not only spiritual leaders, but every individual has a right and duty to find his/her own God that is. Or again turning East. "Look deep within thyself." An amazingly courageous, Eastern-style message from medieval England.

Important To Remember

Our monk in no way intended to suggest that merely reaching the God that is, or Source, is enlightenment. That comes through years of returning again and again, each time bringing greater perception and understanding. Enlightenment, as understood in both East and West, is the gradual gathering of wisdom and knowledge. And that, obviously may not be hurried.

We have devoted this much space to the monk's practices for two reasons. First, although he leans Eastward in his philosophy, he clearly clings to Western concepts in his search for the "God that is." Using his lull-word, God, to bring on the mode and at the same time as a fervent prayer should conclusively prove no need exists, ever, to accept or reject anything.

Also, that same example shows complete fusion of

meditation and religion. And that, for anyone so minded, must be the ultimate. The other extreme, obviously, is no religious connection at all. And that is exactly our point. As the monk advises, you must mold your meditating to suit your needs. Have no fear of departing the usual. Once you have mastered basic meditation, there are no limits on procedure. Indeed, exploring is the most rewarding of all methods. You have seen many procedures. Now devise your own. And while your mind should be open to all ideas, they should remain just that, ideas, to embrace or set aside.

That should clear up any lingering misconceptions about meditation's relation to religion. However, any objective observer must recognize that organized religion does not satisfy needs of every individual. Some never feel comfortable traveling *en masse* down prescribed highways of conventional thinking. So while meditation can be, and often is, used in conjunction with conventional faiths, it also offers an alternative. It is the tough but fulfilling route through that dark cloud of unknowing, for many a naked man/woman, some in determined search for their naked God that is.

COMMENTS AND QUERIES

This chapter may seem superfluous to some. But others will find it of vital importance. And even if you have no interest in religion, it will serve as background material for upcoming chapters. It also should dispel for all time the oft-held notion that meditation is "just another religion."

We should keep in mind that our monk was cloistered in an English monastery at a time when contact with other countries was extremely rare. Yet he manages somehow to appear very Eastern in his approach to so many spiritual matters. How did that come about? We don't have the answer, except to suggest meditation. What's your guess?

While it may not hasten our grasp of meditation methods, this chapter should prove interesting, if for no other reason than that it provides another fascinating mystery. Just one more of meditation's unending array of amazing facts. Be sure to list your reactions.

NOTES

NOTES

IV

Beyond Physical Boundaries

Newcomers tend to regard the claim that meditation can influence situations outside one's mind or body with suspicion, if not outright rejection. Yet most long-time meditators accept it as routine. Surprised? Read on. Surprises abound.

We purposely left this chapter until after discussing the relation of religion to meditation. Members of every spiritual faith hold firm convictions that their prayers, wherever directed, bring results. But advanced meditators around the world are just as certain that meditation, in and of itself, can and does affect people, conditions and events far removed from the meditator's physical influence. And they cite impressive evidence, including personal experience, to buttress their beliefs.

Our 14th century English monk had some thoughts on the subject. As we have seen, he used a unique blend of meditation and prayer which he found to be the shortest, easiest and best route to "the God that is." Here's what he says:

"In a wondrous manner of which you can have no knowledge, all living mankind will be helped . . ."

A Remarkable Claim

He then makes a statement that at first glance seems only vaguely connected. But deeper reflection suggests that quite possibly it is the most important pillar supporting his entire temple of ideas. He says simply, "Love is the power by which all things are united."

As a man of God, he obviously considered love of his God as all important. But remember, he saw God as all inclusive, so such love must be all inclusive. Compassion and caring for one's fellow man, love and devotion between man and wife, parents and children, and for those for whom we are responsible; also concern for all living things and even for our environment in which we all must live. A practical, productive love, all of which falls well within his concept of love for God. This, he believes, is the strongest force for uniting all things!

Aside from its deep and meaningful content, this advice, once again, is amazing. An Englishman of the mid 1300s, tucked away in a monastery, yet sounding for all the world like an Oriental philosopher. "Love is the power by which all things are united," has a distinctly Eastern flavor. Of course, we must not forget that Jesus had much to say on the power of love. So our monk's statement also has impressive Western support.

But still more surprises: When he says, "In a wondrous manner of which you can have no knowledge, all living mankind will be helped," what could he possibly have had in mind but the "sea of energy" with its universal forces, and the ancient Eastern belief that meditators not only receive benefits therefrom, but have an input as well of "positive disturbances"? How could he have known of these perceptions? Did he rediscover them through long years of meditating? Of course, we can never know. Logic, however, suggests there could be no other way. And one further thought: The fact that so credible an authority without reservation refers to the vast powers therein, lends substantial weight for Western consideration.

It should be noted that the concept of "tapping into," then receiving and transmitting mental traffic via the forces, is widely held, and not confined to any one group or region. Stretching across such diverse cultures as ancient Egypt and China, modern India and Polynesia (all well removed from Medieval England) and now much of the West, it is no upstart notion by any measure.

Meditating Doctors

Another interesting phenomenon is the fact that in numerous and widely scattered lands, "doctors" who work solely through meditation are highly respected and sought after as healers. As may be expected, their trade secrets are not generally publicized. From bits and pieces, dropped here and there, however, we gather that their healing meditation is not too different from the usual type.

More detail on this later. We should point out here

that one portion of the exercise on which all practitioners, East and West, agree, is the matter of non-involvement except as a "pipeline." "I have no power," is a common statement. "My function is to conduct or relay the forces to my patients. I'm merely a conduit."

Over and over we find this thought expressed in whatever culture the healer may live and work, leaving no doubt that it is a basic concept.

The Forces

Now that we have had a glimpse of how they are used, let's examine the forces. The ancients obviously could have known nothing about such phenomena except through observation. And even today, it may well be that those forces we do *not* know far outnumber those we do. Of course, we are all familiar with gravity, magnetism, electricity and many more. And without doubt, all these exert influences on the human physical and mental condition. It seems quite likely, however, that most of us never have even considered as a universal force the one our monk puts at the head of the list, love. Is that because the idea is farfetched?

We have seen how the monk regarded love for his God, an all-inclusive caring and compassion. Very like original Buddhist precepts. But there are other methods of expressing love, some of questionable value in the West, but nonetheless impressive.

We have mentioned Dr. Herbert Benson and his extensive work and startling discoveries in the field of meditation. His is primarily a medical interest, but study and research have taken him in all directions and to far places. On one trip, he was invited by the

Dalai Lama to observe Tibetan Buddhist monks in meditation. In a bare room near freezing, they raised skin temperatures, through meditation only, by as much as 15 degrees. Wet, icy towels draped about their shoulders began to steam dry in five minutes or less. Dr. Benson and his team not only watched, they taped and photographed their documentaries. A most impressive proof positive.

To Westerners this sort of thing seems of little value. But since it is routine in many areas, it should serve as an eye-opener. While it is more dramatic and makes a better display, surely the energy and skill used could just as well be directed toward healing, relief of pain or general well-being. If one is possible, so is the other. But these monks consider it a mark of devotion and faith. And as such it is an indisputable proof of love's power. Impressive, but not unique by any means.

By chance (?) this morning's newspaper carries a story of a North Carolina mother who heard terrified screams for help. Racing out her front door, she found her teen-aged son partially pinned under his car. He had been working on it when the jack slipped, dropping the axle onto his hand. Without hesitation, the lady grasped the car's bumper, and mustering strength obviously from some source outside her 110-pound body, she hefted that car high enough to release her son's hand.

Later she said she couldn't recall lifting the vehicle. "She lifted it, all right!" declared her son, who walked away with only a couple of fractured fingers.

Could we find a more convincing example of love's power? She *had* to lift that car. It was crushing her dearly beloved son. But it was impossible. Had she stopped to think, no way could she have done it. But the power of love took charge. We see it, usually not so dramatically, but all around us. Remember the picture from Boy's Town of one lad carrying another piggy-back? "He ain't heavy, Father. He's m' brother," the caption informs us. A power transcending logic or reason.

Amazing Power

You see, when love moves in, there's no room for hate, anger, fear, jealousy, envy or the crippling malice these evils engender. Instead, all our energy is directed toward positive, creative activity. And that's one secret of love's vast power. Clearly, it is also a universal force, the one our monk gives top billing.

But let's return to our theme, the power to influence conditions outside one's own physical area. It seemed desirable first to establish that at least one universal force, love, has undeniable and incredible inherent power. Can that power be directed beyond oneself?

The following few pages may at first glance seem to have little or nothing to do with meditation. But remember, I warned that the advanced version is a total lifestyle. Here's where it begins.

Most of us have been fortunate enough to know at least one person so deeply committed to the love and welfare of his/her fellow creatures that he/she literally moves in an aura of love. I have in mind a dear lady who died many years ago, yet her memory to this day is a pure delight and as clear as though she just stepped out of the room. To be in her presence, to hear her positive, love-filled messages of courage and confidence, was an inspiration. And to those seeking counsel, she listened intently, then offered sage suggestions. I am only one of many whose outlook, values and lifestyle have been vastly enhanced through her influence. Has the power of her love extended beyond her physical presence? Only across deep oceans, wide continents, and many, many years. Yes, love can and does exert amazing power outside one's mind and body.

Using The Forces

So how may we set about using and directing that force? Basics seem obvious. One doesn't plant weeds to harvest wheat. If you wish to project love, first you must develop a field of love. That means digging out those evil, malignant weeds of hate, anger and malice. In their place sow life-enriching, positive forces of love, compassion and good will. Once sown, they will soon grow and thrive into that most potent force in the universe!

Don't expect this to come easily. Most of us have spent a lifetime nurturing a luxuriant field of weeds. Their roots go deep. And the plants have grown so strong and high they form a solid barrier. They keep the good things of life from entering, and they keep our love and caring from reaching out. You will need a gentle but powerful bulldozer of determination to root them out, but you must begin somewhere. Why not at home? Put that splendid brain and spirit to work and note where love could help. Then start making generous applications.

Generosity, incidentally, is one of love's characteristics. But don't equate it with "throwing money at a problem." Wise, selective spending should be one of your aims. But all too often money is not required. Industrial studies have shown that workers value a sense of being needed and appreciated more than added pay. And so do your dear ones. So be generous with kind words. A loving touch, even a smile can be highly effective if it comes from the heart.

Other needs, too, might be filled by giving what costs little but is far more precious than money. Remember the old maxim, "Give a man a fish and you supply a meal. Teach him to fish and you provide meals for a lifetime." Many retirees are sharing experience and know-how with young workers who derive great benefits. But the retirees also gain. Love is a profitable investment!

That's how we begin building that much-needed field of love. But very likely you are way out ahead of me. Your special field probably is flourishing and needs no help from me.

Before leaving this vitally important subject, one more observation: Whatever one's concept of the God that is, it must be closely identified with, perhaps even equated with the forces of the universe. So it should be of immense reassurance when a man of lifelong study and exploration in that realm, our monk, asserts without qualifications, that the most potent of those forces is love. That being the case, we have every reason to expect compassion, caring and concern from the forces. Indeed, we may find new and real significance in the ancient adage, "God is love."

An Unusual Force

This next segment may or may not surprise you. In

any case, it certainly qualifies as vital, close on the heels of love.

Dr. Benson and others have discovered, through careful screening and scientific evaluation, a direct ratio between meditation and realization of the meditator's aim. That ratio is governed by the measure of faith in the outcome. They refer to this surprisingly accurate gauge as the "faith factor."

Of course, true believers have been saying all along that "faith moves mountains," just as meditators have always known "good things happen to meditators." And now we know how we make them happen. We expect them. The simplest, yet perhaps most effective, practical application of the faith factor!

Such impressive evidence is most welcome. But it brings challenge as well as promise. It is said of those Buddhist monks who achieve amazing results through elevated skin temperatures that their most difficult task is maintaining unwavering faith. Without it, they inevitably fail.

This definitely introduces a new element into our meditations. In such undertakings as healing, projecting well-wishes, or any other hope for well-being, it obviously is a vital link. And it throws additional light on the healer and his methods.

It should be apparent that we have here a situation very similar to the concentration-versus-focus problem. Healers or anyone wishing to project well-being obviously must do just that, project. But one must carefully avoid projection of will. Rather, they must be strong transmissions of faith, confidence, KNOWING the desired objective is taking place. A major difference is that faith includes a willingness to accept modified versions of one's desires. Willing, on the other hand, leaves no room for change. Thus it is often totally thwarted, since the hoped-for course may not be possible. So, with that subtle but vitally important distinction in mind, project as strongly as you wish. But make sure it is faith, not will.

Also, we now have an even more pressing reason to feel a genuine exhilaration, to smile from deep within as we meditate. If you have faith in the outcome, why wouldn't you? You do indeed have something to smile about. That cheerful, meaningful, friendly smile will carry over into your lifestyle and infect those around you. Wear it confidently, proudly. It is your badge of identity with two of nature's most potent universal forces: Love and faith!

We have spoken of projecting, but have given very little in the way of clear advice on its use. We did mention that Eastern "doctors" who work with the process seem reluctant to reveal much about their methods. I suspect one reason for this is that their techniques are as varied as are the doctors who practice them. And while we obviously can't describe all, we can offer enough to enable you to work out a process best suited to your own special use.

You will recall that we have suggested sending spirit, then mentally watching, as he brings soothing and healing to an ailing area. That is a widely used procedure, and perfectly sound. And it is universally used to introduce meditators to the healing art. Also, it is faithfully followed by many old-timers. So you need be in no haste to switch. However, you should be aware that it is one of several methods.

Perhaps the most widely practiced is simply taking into one's meditation the desire, need or wish for a specific objective. Then, while enjoying perfectly synchronized relaxation and a euphoric passivity, rest comfortably in the certainty that spirit and universal forces are working to bring about desired ends. In this way, we eliminate distractions of directing or in any way interrupting the session. And after all, isn't it reasonable to assume that the forces are fully knowledgeable of our needs and wishes?

So it should be apparent that these procedures offer a variety of methods, frequently used in combinations. And here, as always, you must work out your own preference from experience and results. Thus, we say again, explore, experiment. Have no fear of the unusual. That's often the most rewarding route!

COMMENTS AND QUERIES

You may have wondered why so much background material is loaded into the foregoing chapter. Well, you should recall two good reasons. First, as we have noted, advanced meditation is more than the act of meditating. It is a total lifestyle. So we must bring to your attention the life a meditator might lead. (Please don't imagine for a moment that we are implying all manage to live up to those lofty standards. It's merely a goal worth shooting for.)

And second, we have pointed out that the major difference between basic and advanced meditating techniques is attitude. But you must know the basis for such advanced attitudes.

So now that you understand its necessity, did it give you any difficulty? Actually, a meditator's lifestyle is the one most of us strive to follow anyway.

We do get into some new material—the "faith factor," and projecting outside one's physical being. These are important items. And while we will have more to say on both, it can do no harm to note here that the method described, taking desires into meditation, then turning them completely over to the forces, is by far the most widely used method of projecting. And small wonder. It is much easier and less likely to inject outside thoughts, thus interrupting the mode.

In this, as with all else in meditation, you must develop your own personal method. But some version of the above should be given close consideration.

And now, as we move into final stages of your meditation studies, be sure to take notes. They'll be invaluable later.

NOTES

NOTES

bling, just set it aside for now. No need to accept or reject. Let meditation and time take care of your perspective. They are powerful and persuasive elixirs.

Another Look At The Great Sea

We have devoted some space to the "Great Sea," that amazing field of pure energy, but not nearly enough. It is vitally important, indeed perhaps the most useful step in advanced meditation. So please be patient if we seem a bit wordy. We must leave no doubt as to its qualities.

Eastern tradition has virtually buried it in ritual and mystery. But digging through that thick sheath, we discover an amazing and deeply revered concept. It holds that through the entire universe spreads an all-encompassing sea of positive energy, the bonding medium that links all the universe into one unit. It is spiritual in nature, realm of the Source, spirits and the forces. It is the origin of creativity, wisdom and knowledge, also source of life's bounties. Yet it is receptive to input from mortals. And, as does everything else in the Eastern scheme of things, it operates within bounds of natural law.

That means that despite its amazing, unseen, largely unknown qualities, it is **not** unapproachable. It is all about us, inescapable, even if we so desired. And we have convincing evidence that it is ever ready and able to serve. But to use it effectively, we generally must understand its unique aspects.

First and foremost, we must realize that not only is it a natural phenomenon, it is nature's highest fulfillment, origin of energy, seat of the Source, and undoubtedly the most important aspect of meditation's many wonders. Also, keep ever in mind that this is not some remote, harsh, unfriendly place. Rather, it is Paradise, Nirvana, the ultimate of wonders and dwelling place of dear friends, family and loved ones. Why, then, would they have any but your best interests at heart? They loved you in life, and they love you now. They are anxious to assist.

This most wondrous and amazing image (or something very close) must be held uppermost in our consciousness whenever we begin our lull-word and call in spirit. He is our link with the Great Sea. As you and he blend, he will help you consciously open your being, allowing the inflow of forces and spiritual power. In this happy state, once you have mastered the simple process, all the benefits and joys of the Great Sea will at last be yours. And it is indeed a simple, easy process.

Now, as you begin your lull-word and bring on the mode, realize that each time you inhale, as you silently pronounce "a-h-h-h," you are drawing in the Great Sea and all its wondrous forces. You are absorbing strength, healing, well-being and infinitely more. You should instantly feel the thrill of increased energy and stamina. Then, as you pronounce your word's second syllable, spirit will help you blend with the Great Sea. As you feel it become part of your being, you should also be aware of forces bringing in its incomparable peace, calm and relaxation.

You see, while the Sea has always been all about you, it has been very like a vast forest in which grow all manner of plants, many full of nourishment. But a wanderer, lost in that forest and unaware of those nourishing plants, may starve while literally stumbling over them. So it is with those who go through life unaware of the Great Sea. In the midst of limitless bounties, they languish in dire poverty, mental and physical. Never again need you suffer such indignities. All those incredible joys and bounties now are yours for the taking!

COMMENTS AND QUERIES

This is our shortest chapter, yet it capsulizes not one, not two, but three important meditation factors. First we find harmonizing with nature explained and detailed. Next we take up spirits and the widely varied concepts in that area. And finally we wade boldly into the Great Sea. Could we find a chapter, of whatever length, more interesting and important?

Our next chapter approaches these subjects in greater depth. But for now, just realize their importance. With these detailed updates, that should offer no problem. It will, however, help prepare you for the upcoming crown jewel, the hope and goal of every serious meditator. Welcome. You have earned it!

And be sure to take notes. Once again, let us point out, your notes will prove invaluable in many, many ways.

NOTES

NOTES

VI

A Wrap-up

This chapter is important because of its nature, tying up loose ends. And in sequence of importance, there is nothing of greater merit than the need to keep constantly in mind that meditation should be FUN. True, we have learned of amazing new aspects. But they're all life-enhancing, richly rewarding. And shouldn't those be fun? So SMILE, you're in meditation! Now to more serious, but still *fun* subjects.

It should be obvious that blending with the Great Sea is a logical method for gaining total benefits. And while new and different, it requires no new thinking or behavior. Just a fully relaxed, passive, receptive stance and awareness of its presence. You know it is pure energy, thus energizing and invigorating. You also know it is the realm of forces and/or spirits, including dear ones. So it obviously is friendly, happy, stressless and rejuvenating. Isn't it then natural and delightful to open up and invite the Sea into our being?

But that must be effortless. Any use of force or will can only hinder. Let nothing interfere with total relaxation and passivity. Allow spirit full control in directing inflow of those major forces. That's a perfect description of blending. It's easy, produces great gains and also permits input of healing, love and faith!

One proof that you are indeed blending is a deeper, more extensive mode. As you find yourself in and of the Great Sea, its vast power and all its other wondrous contents are beginning to flow into your being. This is the ultimate, the greatest of meditation's achievements. So don't expect all benefits instantly. Accomplished meditators spend a lifetime realizing such gains. But each time you return, you will feel greater depth of oneness, total blending, thus far greater powers for well-being, for you and for dear ones. The chief problem in learning to blend with the spirit realm may be that to most of us such contact seems unnatural. But we may have been led to think of spirits or forces as unnatural. So let's explore.

We know many meditators believe the Sea, its forces and/or spirits operate within natural law. So even if we don't accept that theory, let's keep it in mind and assume certain limitations. Don't expect casual conversation from spirits. We know their communication is almost exclusively through thought. So when a useful idea, a helpful hint or any other mental achievement drifts into your consciousness, did it come from nowhere? Is that a logical deduction? Of course not. So why not from the spirit realm? As you begin noting incidents for which some unseen force must be responsible, as you feel their presence ever more keenly, their realm will become easier to accept.

However, as advised, no need to accept or reject. As experiences take you in ever-widening reaches, one day these concepts may take on new significance. Take a page from nature's book—be patient!

And now, as we come to terms with the idea of the Great Sea as a perfectly natural environment of dear friends as well as the entire Spirit Body, it should lose all aspects of the bizarre, the unrealistic. Thus blending with so happy a place should not only be easy, but pure pleasure. Just go totally passive and assume the old wet rag stance, exactly as you blend with anything else. It soon will become not only easier, but vastly more rewarding than any other.

Ever More Wondrous

Wonders of the Great Sea never cease to amaze. One such is the fact that when disaster strikes, those with no knowledge of its properties or even of its existence often reach out in desperation, grasp it and put it to use, without the slightest understanding of how.

That explains such phenomena as the North Carolina woman lifting the car off her son. Also perhaps the remarkable and voluminous feats of Edgar Cayce, "Sleeping Prophet" of Virginia Beach. His heal ing methods, diagnosing, then prescribing simple but amazingly effective remedies for "patients" around the globe, were so well documented that researchers still study them. Yet he always seemed incredulous, never quite sure how such things happened.

Actually, with love leading the list of qualities that make up the forces, it should come as no surprise that compassion and caring may extend outside the ranks of the knowledgeable, offering aid and comfort to those in clear and dire need.

At the other extreme are Eastern yogis, monks, "holy men" and healers. With access to experience gained over thousands of years, they are as knowledgeable on the subject as anyone could ever hope to be. And they routinely demonstrate such skills as raising skin temperature to incredible levels, walking on red-hot coals or broken glass and lying on beds of sharp spikes, all without pain or bloodshed. Some even suspend all physical reactions, taking on aspects of death for long periods. And meditator "doctors" regularly bring healing to "patients" at any distance, through meditation alone. These acts are so commonplace and thoroughly documented that there can be no doubt as to their authenticity.

More Help For You

With such remarkable examples, you no doubt are growing anxious as to just how its magic may be applied to you. Very well. Let us suppose you are suffering from lower back pain, a common complaint among hard-driving Americans. When you begin meditating, get as comfortable as possible. If not too painful, stretch, carefully, Do nothing to aggravate your condition, but follow normal procedure where feasible. Loosen tight clothing, settle into your favorite chair, and begin your lull-word.

Even in pain, your relaxed, passive stance should bring a measure of relief. But the best is just ahead. As you begin, feel the comforting presence of that miraculous Great Sea and its forces. It is washing about, over and through your entire being. And your spirit is there, as always, to help bring the forces into play. As you "watch" his gentle, soothing work over the painful area, discomfort WILL begin to ease and gradually fade away. Just keep meditating, totally passive, relaxed, *knowing* relief is on the way.

Your first try may not be totally successful. But don't despair. Meditation can and WILL chase pain. Even terminal suffering can be eased. But how can you know it's terminal? A doctor's saying so doesn't make it so. Take medication if needed, but KNOW meditation helps, in time may even suffice. Have faith!

That, obviously, is the method for dealing with pain once it has begun. However, in most cases, particularly with such agony as migraine headaches, it is far easier to cope with it before it takes hold.

Migraine and numerous other types of suffering are due in part if not entirely to severe stress, sometimes of unknown origin. So what could be more important than reducing stress and maintaining a stress-free lifestyle? Those subject to any such ailments MUST meditate in "full sessions," twice daily, come what may. And it is very important that they achieve the full mode and *enjoy it.*

Don't think of it as a chore designed merely to chase pain. It is the most pleasant, delightful, easy method of naturally relaxing, thus chasing stress and accompanying tensions, ever discovered. By now you must know that and be enjoying it thoroughly. If not, you're not following the instructions. So, we'll just have to take more stringent measures: More instructions!

We acknowledge redundancy, but plead extenuating circumstances. Of course, it's to impress vital details. But also, we stress different points with each repeat, this time the joy factor. You may have noticed that when you go into meditation in a joyous mood, the

mode comes easily, almost instantly. That's because
our mentality springs naturally toward the happy, the
pleasant. So for heaven's sake, let's "drop all problems
into the cloud of forgetting," hopefully to leave 'em
there. For the session, at least, be a carefree kid again,
no problems of any kind. We have seen that such an
attitude brings solving and healing. So is it worth a
genuine smile? You tell me.

Similar Procedures Elsewhere

We have gone into specifics for chasing pain
because of its obvious importance. To anyone in pain,
all else must wait. But the same general procedure is
just as effective in any endeavor. Problems at the
office? Just go into your mode, dispatch Spirit to take
over, then, while maintaining totally open, relaxed
passivity, feeling the Great Sea's soothing, energizing
effects, EXPECT results. They may take surprising
twists. Radical new ideas may drift into your mentality, the boss may change his demands, any of a thou-
sand solutions are possible. But if you fully expect
positive action, it *will* come. And never forget the
importance played by the "sea." That must be the back-
bone of your meditation modes, always with Spirit's
full participation, from here on.

Any and all such amazing powers are enough to
stir doubt. But when we see them fully documented, or
have personal confirming experiences, doubt is
obviously misplaced. In one area, however, we may
have lingering questions. That is projecting outside
one's physical being.

Such qualms certainly are understandable,
indeed, they are almost certain at first. But let's think

about it. Is it any more incredible than radio or TV broadcasts? Until Marconi developed radio, that idea, too, was a laughing matter. No one laughs now, especially when scientists pick up cosmic emissions that have been en route from distant galaxies for thousands of years.

With mental projections we find ourselves in that same situation. We have all the necessary equipment, including a mentality more complex and capable than any radio or TV apparatus. And we have seen that over the entire universe spreads an all-encompassing sea of positive energy, capable, among other things, of conducting thought waves instantaneously to the most remote areas. So in some respects, we are actually better equipped than are broadcasters.

But don't rely on hearsay: Try it. Strange as it may seem, the easiest of such projections is sending well-being into an ill or grieving friend. To do so, go into meditation holding an awareness of the Great Sea in your conciousness. Also, the fact that your friend needs help. No need to be explicit. Your Spirit knows all needs. Don't clutter the energy waves. And while you must never will anything, it is important that you project positive signals of love and faith. Just *allow* them to "color" your meditation, bringing confidence, joy and anticipation to you, and moving easily through the Great Sea to your friend. They are your "positive disturbances," your input into the universal body of onorgy and croativity. But again, ALLOW them to flow; never force.

As described earlier, many meditator "doctors" enlist the "patient's" cooperation. This may have desirable effects, but I can attest it is not essential. Just meditate, *knowing* the forces are with your friend. Surprisingly simple? True, but effective.

Does It Seem Too Easy

Please don't assume that I am taking a cavalier attitude toward the healing process. No one realizes more fully than I that it is one of, if not *the* greatest skill a meditator can attain. It certainly deserves proper deference. But truly, it *IS* quite simple. We know that the "sea" is a medium through which thought and forces move unimpeded and instantly. We also know that we are an active and fully accepted part of that body. So why wouldn't it accommodate our wishes, either for oneself or a dear one? And at whatever distance? In the spirit world, distance, like time, is of a different dimension. It has little significance in our sense. So you see, if you apply logic and reason to known facts, the process breaks down into easy, fully justifiable expectations. And that, don't forget, is a vital part of the procedure. You MUST EXPECT POSITIVE RESULTS.

Also, what may appear to be failure, may in fact be full success. While instant gratification, as with the woman who found sudden strength to lift the car off her son, does indeed occur, most healing or other positive effects take time. They follow nature's regular course. So how can you tell if you have won? Only time will reveal, often a long time. Nature has a way of going in different directions, frequently directly opposite to one's wishes, to bring results far better than those sought. So again, don't give up simply because there are no immediate signs of success. You may yet bring home the gold. Have patience!

Don't Let Will Interfere

Having discovered such positive power, let us take

steps to avoid interference from negatives. Important to keep ever in mind is the fact that willing, as does concentration, actually hinders, rather than helps realization of your goals. Both tend to prevent the brain's total relaxation, or synchronization. And that, in turn, blocks the mind's full activity (spirit's emergence). So don't get in the way. Strong faith projection is very helpful. Willing can only interfere.

One important reason this is so is because, as noted, we never know in what way the answer to our meditation aims may take shape. I recall a story some years ago in Readers Digest. The writer gave her husband a comic anniversary card, the cover of which read, "You're the answer to my prayer—" Inside it continued, "—not what I prayed for, but the answer to my prayer."

As a girl she had dreamed of a dashing knight in shining armor, pursuing adventure, never a thought for mundane needs of life. In reality, her husband turned out to be a solid, down-to-earth fellow, with all efforts bent toward the well-being of his family. Certainly not what she had prayed for, but the obvious answer to mature prayer. A valuable lesson on nature's mysterious methods tucked away in a comic card.

And an old friend often spoke of his bitter disappointment when, as a boy living in England, a last-minute change of plans caused him and his family to miss their berths aboard the spanking new, "unsinkable" *Titanic*. He lived to a happy, productive, ripe old age. How good it is that our will is not always done!

But let's be perfectly clear. While strong faith projections are vital, willing might easily be mistaken for such. There's a difference, and you must learn to recognize it. Then any worthy desire is possible, if not always the way you planned.

Help From The Spirit World

We have discussed spiritual help in general, but have not gone very far toward describing the more personal type. Many meditators are convinced that help is readily available and forthcoming from spirits and/or the forces. One such manifestation, they believe, comes in some of those "vagrant" thoughts that drift in and out of our consciousness during and after meditation. Since spirits have no physical properties, their chief means of communication—some say their only way—is through thought. So let's not be too hasty in discarding those "idle" or "random" thoughts.

And how may we recognize the real from random? Generally, there is no problem. An answer to a vexing quandary, a long-sought idea for improving a certain difficulty, recall of a forgotten date or important name, all clearly are help from some source. Also, there is one sure-fire method of elimination. You *never* will receive negative or damaging ideas from your spirit or from any other. As noted, all nature is positive, geared totally to development of stronger, more versatile bodies and minds. So reject all negative or harmful thoughts. They're from an animalistic past. Discard and forget 'em!

I wish I could be more specific as to what you may expect. The truth is, there are almost as many experiences as there are meditators. But we can tell what some have been like.

In addition to thought messages, some "see" giant printed, sometimes illuminated, signs. Others hear voices, often those of old friends. A few believe they receive cryptic signals that must be "decoded." But by far the most frequently reported of such phenomena is intuitive knowing, a sudden awareness of a fact without any previous study or exposure thereto.

Incidentally, such messages always are without help from mediums, channelers or other would-be aids. Why should help be required? Would a loved one need a medium to send you a thought? Hardly. So watch for signals. More meditators than you might suppose have learned to use such spiritual assistance. The Buddha, remember, received his vision of a new religion through just such a contact. And thousands of inspirational, business or personal assists are received each day by trusting meditators.

But don't expect miracles often. Spirits generally find opportunities, point the way, even sharpen our wits to help us see them. At some point, however, YOU must take the ball and run with it. You must put to use those opportunities. THEN you may confidently expect more help.

Other Amazing Fields

And that should be sufficient. If you hold an open mind, watchful, sensitive to indications of unseen assistance, and ever alert to thought messages, you should have no difficulty in this phase of advanced meditation. But that is only one of many such phenomena. As we have seen, much—very, very much—of the human brain and mind remain a mystery. True, meditators have learned to use, if not explain, sizable portions. But a vast, unplumbed mass of energy, thought, wisdom and priceless information remains just over our mental horizon. So be bold. Explore. Go confidently into that uncharted universe of the mind. Rewards could shame the wildest dreams of those who sought the "wealth of the Indies." And such exploration easily might qualify as the most rewarding effort any mortal will be privileged to experience in this life.

Small wonder this treasured gem of man's mental accomplishments, this golden secret of the ages, has been so closely guarded, so shrouded in mystery, myth and ritual. This is the ultimate. Once a meditator has achieved this point, his/her aims, of whatever proportions, are within reach. Depth and scope one chooses to plumb are entirely his/her decision. Do you fully grasp the impact of that statement? You can do *anything* you have the faith to do! No longer need you sit helplessly when disaster, illness or misfortune strikes. Now you are equipped to throw your total mentality, backed up by universal forces, into bringing about improvement of any situation. Having enlisted support, through complete harmony with those forces, you are part of an invincible team. Doesn't that knowledge inspire a sense of wonder, amazement, elation? Now you may say in truth, "I am the master of my fate, I am the captain of my soul!" And that, surely, must drive you to deeper exploration and ever-widening understanding and use of your meditation. Good luck, and BON VOYAGE!

COMMENTS AND QUERIES

The foregoing chapter might be considered my notes. It's a tying up of loose ends, a wrap-up. But that in no way should deter your own thoughts and feelings. Jot 'em down while they're fresh.

And as we near the end, we should point out the inclusion of a few note pages at the back of the book. Having traveled through the many phases of meditation, you no doubt have many interesting ideas. Write them down! In this way, you make the book uniquely your own. Best of luck and Happy Meditating, always!

NOTES

NOTES

VII

A String of Pearls

A few years back, an article or book consisting of several items with no transition links was referred to as a "string of pearls." The term was *not* intended to be complimentary. Rather, it implied ineptitude or laziness on the part of the writer.

I believe it will be evident, however, that while the following material is important and certainly should be in any handbook aimed at instructing meditators, these pieces have no logical connecting links. To include them in any of the foregoing chapters would intrude, distract, weaken the message. Therefore, with apologies of sorts, I present a valuable—more than that, a vital—string of pearls.

A "HOW-TO" SESSION

We have discussed so many aspects of meditation that the most important of all might easily get pushed onto a back burner. The "mode" is that item, and let it be stated loud and clear, it is the heart and soul of meditation. Once you have mastered that simple but all-important procedure—bringing on the mode and holding it—your path is clear in whatever direction and to whatever heights you may wish to journey. Without it we drift out of that euphoric state that IS meditating.

This is no big deal. Achieving and holding the mode is almost automatic for experienced meditators. But it does tend to fade. Then intruding thoughts move in, distracting, interrupting. But all we need do is restart our lull-word, bring spirit back, and back comes the mode. But never overlook its vital need at all times. Don't attempt any sort of meditating until you have it firmly fixed in your consciousness. Nothing in all of meditation can work without the mode.

Having said that, surely no more is needed. To paraphrase the noble Bard, "The mode's the thing!" Now, let's move on to other important matters.

One such that might be helpful in "clearing the muddied obvious," is a step-by-step record of a meditation session in progress. I take the liberty here of relating my own experience, since I know exactly how it works.

I begin in the usual fashion, find a comfortable chair, start shucking my cares as though they were worn out old shoes, settle in and relax. It may take a few minutes to calm stress, physical or mental. Then I begin my lull-word *a-h-h-h-h V-o-n-n* in silent, calm, pleasant repetition. And by now a genuine smile is automatic. Almost instantly spirit appears, bringing along the mode—tingling—and the Great Sea. Spirit long ago realized that I need and use the Great Sea in every session, no matter what sort.

The next few minutes are spent luxuriating in that astonishing domain of marvels. I bring into full consciousness a realization of the mystery, amazing power, the limitless potential of this wondrous sea of energy, seat of the Source, realm of forces and/or spirits, including our own dear ones. As the sea envelopes me, moving in and through my total being, there is a sense of incomparable rest and relaxation, of new strength and energy, restoration of worn, tired muscles and nerves. I'm a new person!

It is very hard to leave this delightful sense of total euphoria. Like dragging a child away from Santa. But at some point we must go on to other matters.

If I have aches or pains, I next turn my attention to those. I use the simple method of holding an awareness of spirit and the forces taking over as I watch and project faith. I soon realize my pain is easing and disease or illness gradually fading. Time varies, depending on severity of the pain. I spend enough to fully sense the action and feel a genuine part of it. Once satisfied, I move on.

Next I bring friends or dear ones to mind who may need my help. Rather, I should say, help from the forces. I have no power, but I *can* enlist boundless power of the Great Sea and the forces. This I attempt to do by projecting my full capacity of love and faith to those in need. I spare no effort in this. I image spirit and forces with my dear ones, then send out my strongest mental transmissions of love and faith. But I keep reminding, "no willing, just love, caring and faith." We have seen that this is all important. But it is NOT difficult.

Once again, let us be extremely careful to hold the mode. It's easy, but *all* important.

That's about it. Of course, you need not follow this sequence. If you have other matters you wish to take up, by all means do so, at any point you see fit. Once again, you should, you MUST develop your own system. Just use this as a rough guide, a record of one man's successful meditating procedure. I KNOW yours will be equally succeessful. I'll meditate on it!

Sometime Problems

Most meditators, once they have learned the basic procedure, experience little trouble bringing on the mode. They find it a very pleasant, relaxing process and practice it whenever and wherever possible. But therein lies a possible problem. Under certain conditions some do have difficulty.

One such problem area is lying down. It is so tempting to hop into bed when tired, promising to meditate before dropping off to sleep. But not everyone finds that easy. I am one who is not nearly so apt to go directly into the mode in bed. I've tried to figure out why, but I can only come up with a guess. It may be due to restricted head movement. Or perhaps my body, while relaxed, is not quite so free to stretch and really let go. In any case, I do find it difficult, but not impossible. So in case of illness or other good reason for meditating in bed, I can attest that it can be done. Just expect a tad more trouble gaining the mode.

Also, very important, *never* resort to drugs or alcohol to help bring on the mode. Meditating relaxes, drugs excite. The two are totally incompatible and counterproductive. Besides, meditation has helped many an addict kick the habit for good. So let's be blunt. It can't help but it CAN do untold damage.

Some meditators report trouble bringing on the mode immediately after a heavy meal. I never have had that problem, but since some do, you may prefer to wait an hour or so after eating.

Of course there are many obstacles that may prevent an easy session. But with determination, they CAN be overcome. A young sailor told me a story you might enjoy. He had been on a 48-hour liberty from his ship tied up in Jacksonville, Florida. Like any normal sailor, he had wasted very little time sleeping. He expected to catch a few winks on the last bus out of Daytona Beach that would get him back to his ship on time. So he was not too happy when he boarded and found it crowded, with no seats available. The best spot he could find was clinging to a metal post, hoping to stay awake so as not to drop in the aisle.

To ease the situation, he began meditating. He imaged the Great Sea washing about him, sending energy and strength through his being, energizing his tired, sleepy body. To his pleasant surprise, he did indeed find stamina to remain awake and even enjoy the trip. That was his first experience at using meditation to bring relief in a normal but tough situation. And it came through for him with flying colors.

I can't recall a more compelling endorsement. An exhausted sailor, successfully meditating while hanging from a support bar on a crowded, moving bus! Makes most challenges seem trivial.

So when the going gets rough, put it to the test. The mode may not be as easy to call up as in your favorite chair, with no obstacles to overcome. But it CAN be done. And it WILL do the job. Just one way to find out—try it!

Importance Of Good Health

We're all familiar with the old adage, "A healthy body makes a healthy mind." There's merit in thay saying, although it might be more accurate to phrase it, "A healthy body makes a better connection with a healthy mind."

In any case, good health is important. And one way to gain and hold it is proper exercise. Of course, the type and extent of one's exercise must be tailored to age, physical condition and general lifestyle. Changes into more strenuous activity should be avoided without planning and consultation. Begun and continued in a proper manner, however, exercise is highly desirable and beneficial.

Having said so, let's take a hard look at brutal facts. There are those who, presumably for their own good and valid reasons, simply are not going to exercise. Possibly they are true and faithful believers in Mark Twain's philosophy, "I get my exercise acting as pallbearer for friends who exercise." And like a tree ... they shall not be moved. So to those, I offer a one-word suggestion: Stretch.

It really shouldn't be necessary to urge anyone to stretch. It feels so good, it's a wonder we don't all use every opportunity to do a deep, relaxing s-t-r-e-t-c-h. Ahh, wonderful! And should you need assuring as to its value, just take a look at your cat.

No cat, from the lowly alley variety to the lordly king of the jungle, ever lifts a paw in any unnecessary exercise. Once a good meal has been secured, it's back to sleep. Cats average close to 18 hours of sleep per day. Yet there's no fitter critter to be found than a fat, lazy cat. His secret? Stretching! Totally, exhaustively, luxuriously, before and after each nap and meal. He never misses an opportunity.

You see, stretching, as the word implies, stretches tense, taut muscles and tendons, allowing oxygen to flow in and rebuild tissue. It also causes extra blood to flow into vital organs. Next to meditation, it is perhaps the finest of relaxing tools. So by all means, even if you do exercise, get in the habit of regular stretching. You won't be alone for long. Once friends or coworkers see you enjoying the procedure, they'll try it. And having done so, they're hooked!

Also, another vital and oft-overlooked aid to the good life is deep breathing. It is every bit as important, if not more so, than stretching. But we have included that in our meditating method. So it is to be hoped that it will never be overlooked. However, just in case, please never forget that deep, lung-filling drafts of pure, fresh air, inhaled regularly, is all important.

More On Blending

We have discussed blending and pointed out the importance of using it to bring on one's sense of absolute unity with another entity. It is a simple must in our relationship with spirit. Also, it is a great help when we enlist the Great Sea, either to bring benefits or convey our projections. But blending is so interesting and useful that even though it has limited application to meditation, it seems worth bringing to your attention once more.

We have fully detailed the procedure. So we will only add that it should be a perfectly easy and natural process. We have learned that we are one with the entire universe. So we are merely bringing into our consciousness a realization of conditions as they were meant to be. Unfortunately, most of us have spent much of our lives constructing walls of privacy around our little world. We need to break down such barriers if we would enjoy blending in all its many facets. We think it worth your time because it works toward relaxation, relief of stress and tension, just as does meditation. Here's how it functions. Suppose you are being annoyed by a raucous noise. Just blend totally with it.

Sound like a solution straight out of cuckooland? Actually, I suppose it might be considered an extension of the old saw, "If you can't beat 'em, join 'em." In any case, it's a simple fact that when you blend with *anything*, it becomes easy to endure, even soothing and always interesting. Try it next time you are caught in a traffic jam. Blend with the crowd, sense their anger, frustration, resentment. In so doing, if you are able to truly blend and become a part of the human mass, you will feel a sense of tolerance, of camaraderie, in short, you have blended, become one with that crowd. That seems clearly the explanation of the puzzling "mob psychology."

But you also may use the procedure in more pleasant times and places. A brilliant sunrise, a peaceful wooded glen, an ocean setting, any time you find yourself in happy, interesting surroundings, go into your blending mode. It's an effective and very pleasant way of extending your total harmony with nature.

Obviously, to gain real proficiency, you will need considerable practice. And you may feel that you have better things to do with your time. But some "blenders" engage in very useful procedures. They use the talent to search out truth when dealing with someone they suspect is not quite the above-board, honest John he would have them believe. They claim they are able to blend with his/her mind (spirit), and thus tune in on thought waves (his/her thinking).

I neither attest nor deny these claims. They're for your information and enjoyment only.

Never Force Your Views

A brief suggestion here that may prevent the break-up of beautiful friendships. We have learned never to force anything in meditation. *Allow* the mode to take over, inflowing of the Great Sea and entry of the forces. So it should be with friends or acquaintances.

Once one becomes a proficient meditator and learns first hand of its magic, it is only natural that he/she is tempted to shout it from the housetops. The wish to share with good friends is almost irrepressible. But remember, they have no knowledge of its powers. And how would you feel if someone began exclaiming about some incredible wonder you never heard of?

So be patient. If a friend shows interest, by all means share your precious information. You might casually drop hints from time to time. But if they generate no curiosity, change the subject. Don't be boorish. You will only bring on resentment, bristling determination to have no part of the system.

There is, however, one excellent method of gaining new converts. That is a lifestyle that demonstrates a peace and tranquility transcending ordinary cares and problems. A pleasant, confident smile from deep within that speaks volumes, infects others and invites them to share your priceless secret. Very often they'll ASK about your source of strength and confidence. THEN you may tell them. And they'll listen!

A New Force Abroad

There's a new movement aborning that seems to be growing and may interest you. It is the joining of meditators all over the world in an effort to better conditions throughout our planet.

The idea is to set aside a time each Saturday devoted to meditation focused totally on world peace and well-being. Suggested time is 10 a.m. But if that is not convenient, not to worry. Any time, on the hour, is equally appropriate. You will simply link your forces with that group living in the zone where the time you select prevails.

Group meditation is not new. And it has brought impressive results. Thus, since it requires nothing different except primary focus, and will bring the usual calming, stress-chasing peace and relaxation to you, what have we to lose? If we can bring a measure of reason and sanity to a hate-filled world and secure peace for suffering millions, what a marvelous gift we meditators will present to our less fortunate fellow travelers!

"To All A Good Night"

And finally, what could be more appropriate than a note on slumber? Most meditators have little trouble with insomnia. It usually results from stress, and we should, and most of us do, have stress by the nape of the neck. But there are times when sleeplessness afflicts us all. And when that happens, we have a ready remedy.

First, stretch fully and satisfyingly. Then find a comfortable position and go into your meditation mode, bringing in spirit and the Great Sea. Hold that image, let it completely envelope you, permeate your being, bringing soothing, stress-chasing total comfort. Enjoy its relaxing, calming solace for as long as you like.

In most cases, one will drop off to sleep after a very short period cradled in the quieting reaches of the Great Sea of friendly wonders. But in case sleep refuses to come, so what? A session in such delightful, uplifting, restful company is every bit as energizing and invigorating as sleep, if not more so.

COMMENTS AND QUERIES

Well, I hope you agree the foregoing material is important enough to warrant flouting conventional wisdom concerning a "string of pearls." Such matters as exercise, stretching, deep breathing, in fact all of 'em, seemed so to me.

You may feel that notes on so wide-ranging a list are hardly necessary. But once again, may we urge that you jot down any ideas, problems or experiences that depart the norm. While they may seem trivial, they will be most helpful in reconstructing your progress, for your own benefit or that of a friend who at some future date may use your book.

And since this is the last of the Comments and Queries, I'll just add a fervent hope that they will be as helpful as my judgment suggests. As noted, writing out thoughts and ideas is the finest possible way of fully developing, then stamping them firmly in one's mentality. Also, what could more effectively make this book uniquely your own than helping write it? Good luck. May your ideas blossom like flowers in early spring!

NOTES

NOTES

VIII

In Self-Defense

That pretty well wraps it up except for one small afterthought. When I began this book, I fully intended to follow every good reporter's practice, relating only facts, keeping my views completely apart. But very early I realized that was not going to work. Here's why.

After 30-something years in the newspaper business, with freelancing magazine work, reams of ad copy and even a bit of "ghosting," a simple little expose seemed like a piece of cake. But within days of starting my research, in my very first try at bringing on the mode, I knew this was going to be a totally new and much deeper job than anything I had ever tackled. Far from "a simple little expose," I had stumbled onto one of man's most amazing endowments. It still holds me in awe. And rare is the day I fail to discover some new wonder. But one of the oddest of my early discoveries was its relative obscurity in the West. So I decided to set about changing that, to bring it to America's attention in clear, uncluttered fashion.

And so I hereby apologize, sorta, for getting so deeply involved. But you see, I had to do whatever was needed. I had to make thoroughly clear its incredible powers, much of it uncovered through personal experience. Thus, since I have so freely offered views and comments, you certainly have every right to know more about me. Here's a rundown.

I suppose it should be stated up front that I am not a member of any organized religion, philosophical or other such group. My leanings are a kind of eclectic East-West compromise. I find the Creative Intelligence concept fully acceptable. And long ago, before I learned that it is part of Eastern thinking, I concluded that full use of one's brain and mind is the only reasonable expression of respect and veneration. I also subscribe wholeheartedly to the theory of universal oneness. It explains, at least to my satisfaction, so many cosmic mysteries. And knowing that my spirit, and yours, are part of the Great Spirit Body is an awesome, elevating realization. It implies vast responsibilities as well as manifest benefits.

We have touched on the subject of spirits joining or merging, while in some manner maintaining an individuality. Also, perhaps revisiting earth in another life. I think they probably do. But frankly, I don't see that such details make the slightest difference. How can they affect us? One thing I do have strong feelings about, however, is their watching over and providing guidance and protection for their living loved ones. I firmly believe they do, my silent partners—and yours.

I base this conviction on two persuasive factors: 1) Why shouldn't those who loved us in life continue to do so after death, providing whatever aid and comfort they can? I would not expect to be shoved bodily out of the path of an on-rushing truck. But they might plant a desire in my mind to turn and glance into a shop window, rather than step off the curb.

And 2) That sort of thing has happened to me so many times that only a dire idiot could miss its significance. Coincidence? OK. But please, good spirits, keep those coincidences working!

As to details of spirit activity, I refuse to fall into that annoying trait of "explaining" everything, including what one does not and cannot know anything about. I take comfort from Hamlet's remark: "There are more things in heaven and earth, Horatio, than are dreamt of in your philosophy." Meditation can disclose much. And what's left should be a pleasant surprise when we finally turn in for recycling.

One troubling question perhaps should be briefly discussed, our relation to our own spirit. If we are indeed each a part of the Spirit Body, by virtue of our spirit's relationship, how may we explain the crime, senseless destruction and wanton cruelty all about us? Well, we may or may not be bonded to spirit at birth. Certain it is that at every step along life's journey, we make a choice. We may take the high road of spirit, or choose the animal instincts left in our makeup from earlier stages of development. Obviously, one who disdains counseling of spirit grows away from spirit. Those who strive to use and continually expand mental prowess just as obviously achieve a closer relationship, eventually an actual bonding or "enlightenment." So it must be apparent that when death releases the spirit, those who have willfully spent their days in crime, destruction and degradation remain on the lower level they have chosen. Those who have sought the way of spirit will become a part of spirit, and at death enter the spirit world as part of that body.

I rather suspect a sense of this state of affairs in the minds of ancients gave rise to the heaven-hell concept. Then, over the ages, for clear and obvious reasons of self-serving, various priesthoods expanded the theory in amazing directions.

On the subject of prayer, I am one who feels that advanced meditation is the epitome of prayer. How else could one view an earnest attempt to find and know the Source? But let me stress again, use any method that suits your taste, so long as it is an honest attempt to reach pure truth. I sincerely believe honesty, courage of one's convictions and faith in the outcome are basics that bring success to meditation and/or prayer. I cite our 14th century monk as my authority. But test it. I did.

We have discussed the power of love as one of the forces of the universe that make up that all-powerful energy field. I fully subscribe to our monk's statement, "Love is the power that unites all things." That clearly covers the power to heal and make whole. And I have personally seen such convincing evidence of that power that it no longer poses any doubt in my mind.

And finally, let's try to answer a question that may bother many. We have stated that meditation is not a religion. Very well, just what is it? You have every right to ask. But since so many non-meditators, those who, for the most part, know nothing about it, have called it so many unflattering things, and even long-time meditators can't agree, finding a clear definition is no easy task. Those dedicated to pure science often insist the subconscious is capable, therefore probably responsible for most of meditation's wonders. More widely held is the belief that outside spiritual influence is clearly evident. And then there are those who say, in effect, "Let's leave the 'who' and 'why' to philosophers. We know 'what' happens and 'how' to make it happen. That's enough for us."

That is exactly as it should be. We have noted that meditation is a personal thing. Like a skillfully cut and polished diamond, it displays beautiful but differing facets to each viewer. And so we offer the following, in an effort to cover, but never to smother:

"Meditation is a blend of science and philosophy. It seeks to gain, then apply knowledge to better understand and use our brain and mind. Basic meditation employs synchronization of the brain to bring total mental and physical relaxation, thus better health. Advanced meditation reaches into the metaphysical, and through absolute harmony with nature, enlists all-powerful forces of the universe to cleanse, heal and lift toward a higher level of understanding."

That might be termed our "dictionary definition." But all experienced meditators know it's much more than that. The real definition, the one that only time can reveal, is far more encompassing and virtually impossible to put into words. But let's venture where angels fear to tread and make a feeble effort.

It's suddenly realizing a great truth, one that for some inexplicable reason has never crossed your mind. It is coming upon an obvious answer to a long-time problem. It is discovering an unexpected strength and know-how to accomplish a task that only a short time ago was impossible, and a positive knowledge that some force, unknown and unseen, has offered help. But perhaps most important is the attitude of unruffled acceptance of such things as normal and natural.

Dr. Howard Gardner has offered a scientific explanation, as reported in our section on basic meditation. He believes that opening our intelligence to all of its seven types, as we do with brain synchronization, makes far more available one's total mental potential. And he certainly makes an excellent case. But meditators know intuitively that more is involved. In time, no doubt, science will provide answers. For now, however, why not go with the advice of our 14th century monk regarding the lull-word, "Just use it. Don't mess around with it."?

By all means use meditation. Explore, experiment. Through amazing, mysterious power of the Great Sea, feel actual blending of mortal and spiritual mentality. The lull-word is your magic wand and a satisfying, comforting role in universal creativity awaits you. Then one day, having ventured through that wondrous realm, perhaps *you* will define it.

And now, may the forces be with you evermore, and may your meditations bring peace, harmony, wellbeing and, if you so desire, enlightenment.

ALOHA!

Acknowledgements And Thanks

First, to those ancient unknown explorers who discovered and developed meditation. To them the entire human family owes a deep debt of gratitude. Through their pioneering efforts untold suffering and anxiety have been eased or eliminated. They must indeed have been spiritually inspired.

Next, to the anonymous 14th century English monk who, despite real and imminent danger of death at the stake for heresy, boldly proceeded to write his book, THE CLOUD OF UNKNOWING. From it we glean so much of our basic and advanced meditation procedure.

Also, to Ira Progoff, whose book by the same name steered me to the original. Special thanks for his deep and penetrating commentary. He points up vital between-the-lines meanings and messages without which much of the book's impact would be lost.

And to Dr. Herbert Benson, whose revealing scientific studies of meditation techniques have led to vital new perceptions and development of improved methods.

To Steve McLachlin, staff artist with The Daytona Beach News-Journal, for his unusual treatment that brings life to our cover and the cover to life. A clear example of art that expresses more clearly than words.

Also, to Michael Arman and Katherine Keegan of Ormond Beach, Florida, whose valuable assistance in proofing, layout and planning the book's format has made it more easily read and understood, thus more useful. Could anything be more important?

And most certainly to all those generous and patient "guinea pigs" who so stoically endured my probing, relentless questions into their meditating methods, reasoning and results. They are far too numerous to name, but to one and all, my deepest thanks.

And finally, to you, the reader, without whom there would be no need for, and thus, no book.

To all, my most hearty gratitude.

Order Form

REVEILLE BOOKS
Post Office Box 3114
Ormond Beach, FL 32175

Please send me the following:

_____ Complete No-Frills Meditation for Americans On-The-Go at $7.95 each, plus $1 postage for the first book and 50 cents postage for each additional book.

Check or money order, please.

Name _____

Address _____

City, State, Zip _____

Please print or type!

Order Form

REVEILLE BOOKS
Post Office Box 3114
Ormond Beach, FL 32175

Please send me the following:

_____ Complete No-Frills Meditation for Americans On-The-Go at $7.95 each, plus $1 postage for the first book and 50 cents postage for each additional book.

Check or money order, please.

Name _____

Address _____

City, State, Zip _____

Please print or type!